"The celebrities and chefs featured in this cookbook have come together
to create one of the most interesting combinations of culinary art and
entertainment wrapped together in the same book."
— Chef Mark Ellman —

"Every time you create meals from one of the recipes in this book, you can
take comfort in not only the food but in knowing you made a contribution
toward a very worthwhile cause."
— Diana Krall —

"Reading these often personal family recipes and notes from the celebrities
and chefs makes you feel like you know each one of them personally."
— Chef Roberto Donna —

A "great book for a great cause."
— Tommy Tune —

"Truly a collector's book with page after page of great recipes and photos of
your favorite stars and chefs."
— Chef Guy Martin —

"An entertaining book to cook from and enjoy."
— Lane Brody —

"Look at it this way: by buying this book, you're helping in the fight
against AIDS, and you get to find out what the famous celebrities like
to eat in their own homes."
— Chef Raymond Blanc —

Celebrity Cookbook

RECIPES FOR A CURE

COMPILED BY
– LISA ANN –

Carrington Publishing
NEWPORT BEACH, CA

Published by Carrington Publishing
P.O. Box 1424
Newport Beach, CA 92659

Publisher's Cataloging-in-Publication Data

Celebrity cookbook: recipes for a cure/compiled by Lisa Ann --
Newport Beach, CA : Carrington Publishing, 2004.

p. ; cm.
ISBN 0-9726433-0-3

1. Cookery. I. Carrington, Lisa Ann.

TX714.C66 2004   2003100539
641.5--dc21   0306

Project coordination by Jenkins Group, Inc. • www.bookpublishing.com
Cover design by Kelli Leader
Interior design by Chad Miller/Fourteen Little Men, Inc.

08 07 06 05 04 • 5 4 3 2 1

Printed in Italy

DEDICATION

To all who support and work
in AIDS research and awareness …
You are an inspiration!

REMEMBRANCE

Bill Blass

George Burns

Maurice Gibb

Douglas Fairbanks Jr.

Dorothy Lamour

David Lewis

Dudley Moore

Bob Hope

Gene Kelly

CONTENTS

STARTERS, SOUPS, & SALADS

VEGETABLES & PASTA

MEATS, POULTRY, & FISH

DESSERTS

THIS 'N' THAT

FOREWORD

It is an honor, and it is with great pride that I represent the extraordinary number of outstanding celebrities, sports stars, famous personalities, artists, and renowned chefs contributing to this wonderful cookbook.

It is very symbolic that this amazing collection of varied recipes for the preparation of food, the staff of life, assists in the financing of research to save lives. One of the foundations of civilization, of man's humanity to man, is the providing of food to friends at a dining room table as well as to strangers who knock on a door. The AIDS crisis has motivated all of us to work together to provide help for our AIDS-stricken friends and strangers.

For this cookbook, we contributed recipes. As long as the search for a cure is needed, we will continue donating as much time and as much energy as possible.

I'm very grateful to Lisa Ann for her leadership and her devotion to the battle against AIDS and for authoring this book.

We salute you, the purchasers and readers of the *Celebrity Cookbook,* and we congratulate you for joining one of the most important battles facing society today—finding a cure for a terrible illness.

From all of us, our sincere thanks.

Beverly Garland

ACKNOWLEDGMENTS

My sincere gratitude to Beverly Garland for her generous support and for contributing the foreword and to Gene Walsh for facilitating this project.

Thank you to all the wonderful chefs who took time away from their kitchens to send me their favorite recipes. Chef Jean-Pierre Dubray of the Ritz Carlton in San Francisco, you were the first to contribute a recipe. Thank you for getting the wooden spoon mixing!

Chef Alessandro Strata, I'm looking forward to tasting your cuisine the next time I'm in Las Vegas at Renoir. Thank you for your support.

Chef Mark Ellman, Maui Tacos, for always responding to my questions and for sharing your special pictures of your celebrity friends who enjoy Maui Tacos. It's been fun having you as part of this book. See you in Hawaii next time I'm there and best wishes on your new restaurant.

Chef Hubert Keller, thank you for sending me such an impressive media package and an outstanding truffle recipe. Thank you also for sharing the photo of yourself with President Clinton.

Many thanks to all the other talented chefs who wrote me such wonderful letters and donated great recipes.

To Siegfried & Roy, thank you for the royal treatment at your Vegas show. You truly are magical!

Thank you also to the wonderful Tommy Tune for your beautiful letter and support for this book.

To Michelle Krall, thank you for your support and for sending everything on behalf of your sister Diana.

To Darice O'Mara, thank you for your lovely letter and for sending me Mr. Paul Newman's recipe.

To Donald Trump, thank you for your encouraging letter.

To Dallas Raines, thank you for giving this book "blue skies" throughout.

To Bob Robbins of the Jenkins Group, thank you for your constant support and for generously sharing your knowledge throughout this project.

To National AIDS Fund, thank you for all the heartwarming efforts you produce 24/7 to make a difference toward AIDS. I feel honored to have my book associated with such a rewarding and dedicated team especially Kandy, Lissa, and Michael.

A special thanks to Jerrold Jenkins and the entire staff at the Jenkins Group for understanding my vision, for all your hard work, and for putting me in touch with Jon Roth of Brightbridge Communications, the website designer.

I would also like to thank Leo Vortouni for his invaluable help, support, and encouragement throughout this project. Without him, this book may not have been finished.

And to all the celebrities who took time out of their busy schedules to support this project. I was honored by all your letters, phone calls, and e-mails. I can't express my appreciation sufficiently to all of you.

INTRODUCTION

I am delighted to offer you the *Celebrity Cookbook* with more than 100 recipes, photos, and autographs donated by favorite celebrities and star chefs.

I created this book to share with you what these famous personalities like to cook and eat. It has been a rewarding experience for me from beginning to end. I have devoted my time and enthusiasm during the past four years in collecting and selecting, along with tasting, the recipes that went into this book.

It has been a full-time effort on my part to make the cookbook a success. It was also a longtime goal of mine to create a book that involved cooking combined with a worthwhile cause.

Being able to donate part of the proceeds of this project to the National AIDS Fund is a great honor. The overwhelming response I received from the entertainment industry and the chefs went far beyond what I had imagined.

The question I get asked most often is, "Why did the celebrities take time to share their recipes?" They all wanted to do something for an important cause and, at the same time, contribute to an entertaining cookbook.

The variety of the recipes is what makes this book so much fun. There is something for everyone: from simple, health-conscious to gourmet recipes. Discovering the exceptional dishes that make up this book will definitely whet your appetite.

I propose you host your own celebrity dinner party by preparing recipes from your favorites in this book. Your guests will be in for a fun-filled evening. Check the Web site (www.BonAppetitwithCelebrities.com) for suggestions.

Write me with your comments, I would like to hear from you.
carringtonpub@adelphia.net

Lisa Ann

The following is a favorite recipe of mine that I often prepare:

Vanilla Rum French Toast

This is the best French toast you ever tasted! It's great served on Sunday mornings, and I like to serve it with Ramos Fizz. It's really a treat. Enjoy!

INGREDIENTS

1 stick (½ cup) unsalted butter
1 ¼ cup packed dark brown sugar
2 tablespoons corn syrup
6 1-inch-thick slices of baguette or challah bread, trim crusts and make sure bread is day old (I slice my bread and remove crusts and leave out for at least two days to dry)
5 large eggs
1 ½ cups half-and-half
1 tablespoon heavy cream
1 teaspoon almond extract
4 teaspoons vanilla rum
¼ teaspoon salt

PREPARE ONE DAY AHEAD

- In a small saucepan melt butter with brown sugar and corn syrup over medium heat, stirring until smooth and pour into a 13 x 9 x 2-inch baking dish. Arrange bread slices on syrup in one layer.
- Wisk together eggs, half-and-half, heavy cream, almond extract, vanilla rum, and salt until well combined and pour evenly over bread. Cover and chill overnight.
- Preheat oven to 350°F and bake uncovered until edges are golden, about 40 minutes depending on oven. Serve French toast immediately.

Serves 2.

Celebrity Cookbook

RECIPES FOR A CURE

STARTERS, SOUPS, & SALADS

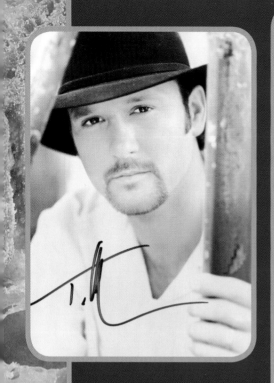

Tim McGraw's Favorite Cheese Grit Recipe

Boil according to the directions on the grit box:

3 cups water
¾ cup grits
1 teaspoon salt

Add:

1 8-ounce package Velveeta
1 stick softened margarine
2 beaten eggs

DIRECTIONS

- Mix well.
- Add 1 small can El Paso chopped chilies and mix well.
- Pour into a greased casserole dish and bake at 350°F for 45 minutes.

4

– MARTINA MCBRIDE –

Tortilla Soup

INGREDIENTS

1 large onion, chopped
8 garlic cloves, minced
6 tablespoons vegetable oil, plus additional
  for frying tortillas
7 green chilies, stemmed and seeded
4 cups water
5 tomatoes, seeded and chopped
8 cups chicken broth
Salt and pepper to taste
12 corn tortillas, cut into strips
1 ½ cups shredded Monterey Jack cheese
2 avocados

DIRECTIONS

- In a stockpot, cook onion and garlic in
  4 tablespoons oil over medium heat, stirring
  until soft. Increase heat and add chilies, stirring
  to avoid burning. Cook for 1 minute or until
  soft. Remove one chile and cut into 10 strips;
  reserve for garnish.
- To the pot, add 4 cups water and tomatoes and
  bring the liquid to a boil. Simmer mixture for
  30 minutes.
- In a blender, purée the mixture in batches.
- In a pot, heat 2 tablespoons of remaining oil over
  medium heat until hot but not smoking. Return
  the purée and cook, stirring for 5 minutes. Stir
  in broth, salt, and pepper. Simmer soup for
  15 minutes.
- In a large skillet, heat ½ of additional oil over
  high heat until hot but not smoking. Fry the
  tortilla strips in batches, stirring for 30 seconds
  until crisp. Transfer to paper towels to drain.
- Divide fried tortillas among 10 heated bowls.
  Pour the soup over them and top each one with
  one strip of the reserved chile. Sprinkle each
  serving with some shredded cheese and top soup
  with sliced avocado wedges. Note: the avocado
  is optional. This recipe can easily be halved or
  doubled.

Tina's Favorite Salad

INGREDIENTS

½ head crisp romaine lettuce, cut in small bite-sized pieces

1 sweet tomato, chopped

½ cup fresh green peas or corn kernels

1 stalk celery, cut small

1 carrot, cut small

½ green pepper, cut small

¼ onion, chopped small

½ cup fresh string beans (already steamed 4 minutes and refrigerated to cool), cut into small pieces

1 handful chopped walnuts

½ ounce raisins (black, small single-serving-size box)

Dressing:

2 tablespoons balsamic vinegar

1 teaspoon olive oil

1 teaspoon Dijon mustard

Dash cayenne pepper

DIRECTIONS

· Mix all veggies together.

· Prepare dressing and pour over salad.

– PETER YARROW –

Puff's Favorite Salad

INGREDIENTS

Salad:

1 small tin of light tuna fish in water
2 tomatoes, cut in eighths
1 cucumber, sliced and peeled
1 head Boston or romaine lettuce
8 radishes, cut in halves
2 Belgian endives

Dressing:

¾ cup extra-virgin olive oil
¼ cup balsamic vinegar
2 tablespoons Dijon mustard
4 drops Tabasco sauce
1 teaspoon Worcestershire sauce
1 large clove garlic, crushed
1 teaspoon fresh lemon juice
¼ cup finely grated Romano or Parmesan cheese

This is an old recipe, but most assuredly a favorite! Plus, as you can see, it utilizes something by the sea. Best wishes ...
Peter Yarrow

DIRECTIONS

For Salad:

- Wash and spin-dry lettuce.
- Tear lettuce into medium-sized pieces.
- Cut tomatoes and set aside.
- Slice cucumber.
- Separate leaves of endive.
- Combine lettuce, endive, cucumber, radishes, and tuna in bowl.

For Dressing:

- Crush garlic and let steep in the ¾ cup olive oil for ½ hour.
- Remove garlic from olive oil; discard garlic.
- Combine balsamic vinegar and mustard. Gradually add olive oil, stirring constantly so ingredients do not separate.
- Add remaining dressing ingredients (except cheese) and mix well with fork.
- Add tomatoes and dressing to salad and toss gently.
- Sprinkle with finely grated Romano or Parmesan cheese and serve.

Enjoy my favorite dish!

– PAUL ANKA –

Warm Scallops and Avocado Salad

INGREDIENTS

2 cups homemade chicken broth
¾ cup sea scallops
1 ½ tablespoons sherry wine vinegar
1 teaspoon Dijon mustard
Salt and freshly ground pepper
2 platefuls fresh spinach, cut in a chiffonade or thin strips
1 avocado, sliced and sprinkled with lemon juice
Toasted walnuts

DIRECTIONS

- Heat broth to a high simmer; do not boil. Add scallops, cover, and cook until just barely done, about 2 or 3 minutes. Turn off heat and pour scallops and broth into a bowl that has been set into another bowl of ice all the way up the sides. Set aside until ready to assemble salad.
- Meanwhile, in a small saucepan, combine olive oil, sherry wine vinegar, Dijon mustard, and season to taste. Heat to simmer.
- Just before serving, remove scallops from broth and slice thinly into rounds. Make a bed of spinach on each of the 2 plates. Arrange avocados in a star pattern over spinach. Arrange scallops atop avocados, sprinkle with walnuts, and pour hot dressing over all. Serve at once.

Yields 2 servings.

Strawberry Salad©

INGREDIENTS

1 cup boiling water
2 3-ounce packages strawberry jello
1 20-ounce can crushed pineapple, drained
2 pints frozen strawberries, thawed
3 bananas (ripe)
16 ounces sour cream
1 cup nuts (your favorite)

DIRECTIONS

- Dissolve jello in boiling water.
- Mash bananas.
- Drain pineapple.
- Mix with nuts and strawberries; add to jello. Put ½ of mixture in bowl and let gel. Spread sour cream over this. Pour remaining jello over all and return to refrigerator until firmly set.

Randy Travis

Best wishes!

Something for a Sunday breakfast! Enjoy!

– STEPHEN BISHOP –

Martian Eggs

INGREDIENTS

3 eggs or eggbeaters
¼ cup chopped chives
Nonfat milk
¼ cup grated cheddar cheese or ¼ cup grated
   soy cheese
Sour cream or soy sour cream
Salsa
¼ avocado

DIRECTIONS

- Place eggs in blender with chopped chives. Blend well until mixture turns green. Put mixture into skillet with 2 tablespoons of nonfat milk and cook for a few minutes. Season with your choice of seasoning.
- Place eggs on plate and sprinkle with cheese, avocado, a teaspoon or two of salsa, and a dab of sour cream. Presto—"Martian Eggs"!

– PAT SAJAK –

Gin Fizz Egg Pie

INGREDIENTS

6 strips thick bacon
1 onion, diced
1 28-ounce can peeled tomatoes
10 fresh mushrooms, sliced
2 cans Vienna sausages, cut into ¼-inch slices
6 slices Jack or American cheese
1 dozen eggs
½ cup fresh cream
Parmesan cheese
Pimento strips
Sour cream
A shaker of gin fizzes

DIRECTIONS

· Cut bacon into 1-inch pieces; fry until crisp
  in a large ovenproof skillet. Pour off most of
  grease; brown onions in rest. Mix in tomatoes,
  mushrooms, and sausages; let simmer 15
  minutes. During last minutes, stir in
  cheese slices.
· Gently beat eggs with cream and stir into pan
  mixture. Bake at 350°F for 30 minutes or until
  eggs have cooked to a nice golden crust.
  For last 5 minutes, sprinkle Parmesan cheese
  over crust.

SERVING SUGGESTIONS

· Mix a shaker of gin fizzes on entry of pan into
  oven and enjoy until eggs are done. Serve eggs in
  pie slices, garnished with thin strips of pimento
  on each slice, along with a bowl of sour cream for
  those who desire this final touch.

My Kids' Favorite Scrambled Eggs

INGREDIENTS AND INSTRUCTIONS

- Break 4 eggs into a bowl and discard the shells.
- Add 2 capfuls of vanilla extract and a sprinkle of garlic salt.
- Mix well until frothy and set aside.
- Lightly coat the bottom and sides of a skillet with butter or margarine. Heat the skillet on medium heat and add the egg mixture. Stir until the eggs are still loose and not quite cooked. (Optional: add Parmesan cheese to taste.) Remove from the heat and allow to set approximately 30 to 45 seconds to finish cooking. Serve immediately.

Feeds 2 to 3 people.

This recipe is the one thing my kids say I can cook better than their mom, so I'm sending it for all the other dads to whip up some morning …

I'm happy to contribute to this cookbook and wish you the best of success!

– JAMES MITCHELL –

Eggs Olé

INGREDIENTS

1 dozen eggs

2 cups sour cream

1 can Ortega peeled green peppers, seeds removed

1 pound Monterey Jack cheese (you won't need that much, but get it)

Salt and pepper

DIRECTIONS

· Preheat oven to 350°F.

· Oil lightly a 12 x 9 x 2-inch Pyrex dish. Lay peppers on bottom to cover, opening them up. Cover peppers with thin slices of cheese.

· Beat eggs and combine with sour cream, salt, and pepper, mixing well. Pour over peppers and cheese. Bake in oven for 30 minutes.

This recipe is from my Mexican American sister-in-law.

The recipe is Tex–Mex and is shunned by most—all those eggs, cheese, and sour cream! But it's delicious for a late breakfast or brunch …

I'm delighted to share this recipe with you. Enjoy!

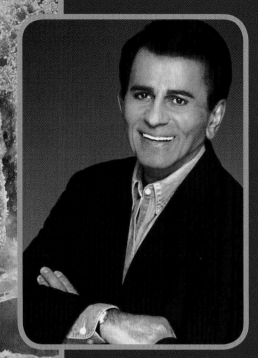

14

– CASEY KASEM –

Vegetarian Soup

INGREDIENTS

2 cups of water

1 box frozen green beans (or ¾ pound fresh green beans)

½ large (or 1 whole small) cauliflower, cut into florets

3 large chopped carrots

4 large chopped zucchinis

6 stalks sliced celery

2 to 4 large yellow onions or a 12-ounce bag of frozen chopped onions

1 16-ounce can peeled tomatoes

1 46-ounce bottle or can of V-8 juice

½ teaspoon thyme

DIRECTIONS

- Mix all ingredients, bring to a boil, and simmer for 15 minutes. This recipe makes a large pot of soup that will keep for 2 weeks in the refrigerator, covered.

– BARBARA BUSH –

Zucchini Soup

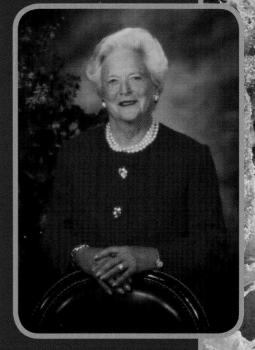

INGREDIENTS

1 pound cleaned, unpeeled zucchini
1 ¾ cups chicken broth
2 tablespoons shallots (often, I use onion or leeks)
1 clove garlic, minced
1 teaspoon curry powder
½ teaspoon salt
½ cup coffee cream

DIRECTIONS

- Chop unpeeled zucchini, shallots, and garlic.
  Put all 3 in a heavy skillet and cook for 10 to 20
  minutes. Stir to keep from burning.
- Put all ingredients in blender and blend.
  Add cream.
- Serve hot with croutons or cold with chives.
  Freezes well. I would freeze without cream and
  add the cream later.

Serves 6.

Barbara Bush

*This is a family favorite—
we serve this a lot in
Kennebunkport.*

*Serve with a nice salad and
English muffins for a delicious
light lunch.*

Enjoy!

Wild Mushroom Bisque

Prep: 3 minutes
Cook: 10 minutes

INGREDIENTS

2 tablespoons butter or vegetable oil
3 ounces shiitake mushrooms, chopped
2 tablespoons minced shallots
1 10 ¾-ounce can condensed cream of mushroom soup
1 14 ¾-ounce can beef broth
1 cup half-and-half
2 tablespoons sherry
⅛ teaspoon freshly ground pepper

DIRECTIONS

· In a large saucepan melt butter or oil. Add mushrooms and shallots, cooking over medium heat, stirring frequently until softened, about 5 minutes.
· Raise heat to high and whisk in condensed mushroom soup, beef broth, and half-and-half. Bring to a boil, reduce heat to medium low, and simmer uncovered 5 minutes. Just before serving, stir in sherry and season with pepper.

Mexicale Hot Stuff Party Din-Din

Phyllis Diller

INGREDIENTS

1 ½ pounds ground beef
1 medium onion, diced
1 can creamed style corn
1 10 ½-ounce can tomatoes with green chiles
1 8-ounce can enchilada sauce
8 ounces grated cheddar cheese
1 4-ounce can sliced ripe olives
Diced green chiles, oregano, cumin, garlic powder
   to taste
6 large tortillas
1 cup grated jack cheese

DIRECTIONS

· Brown ground beef, stirring to keep meat
  crumbly.
· Combine ground beef with onion, creamed
  corn, tomatoes with green chiles, enchilada
  sauce, cheddar cheese, ripe olives, and diced
  green chiles, oregano, cumin, and garlic powder
  to taste.
· Tear 3 tortillas into pieces and spread over the
  bottom of an 11 x 7 x 2-inch baking dish. Spread
  ½ the meat mixture over the tortillas. Tear
  remaining tortillas and spread over meat mixture.
  Top with remaining meat mixture. Sprinkle with
  jack cheese. Bake at 325°F for 30 minutes.

Makes 8 to 10 servings.

My best wishes,
Rosalynn Carter

Plains Special Cheese Ring

INGREDIENTS

1 pound grated sharp cheddar cheese
1 cup mayonnaise
1 cup chopped nuts
1 small onion, grated
Black pepper to taste
Dash of cayenne

DIRECTIONS

- Mix the above ingredients and mold with hands into desired shape (I mold into a ring) and place in refrigerator until chilled.
- To serve, fill center with strawberry preserves. Can be served as a complement to a main meal or as an hors d'oeuvre with crackers.

Cottage Cheese Salad

INGREDIENTS

1 3-ounce box jello (I use lime flavored)
1 32-ounce container plain cottage cheese
1 8-ounce can crushed pineapple (in its own juice)
1 8-ounce container Cool Whip whipped topping (regular or lite)

DIRECTIONS

- In a bowl put cottage cheese and then pour dry jello mix right from the box over it. Mix well.
- Drain pineapple and then add pineapple to mixture. Fold in Cool Whip. Refrigerate until ready to serve. You can also add chopped walnuts or pecans if desired.

Vanna White

Cream of Butternut Squash and Sage Soup

INGREDIENTS

4 tablespoons unsalted butter
1 small chopped onion
½ teaspoon chopped garlic
3 cups butternut squash (peeled, cut in half and seeded, chopped)
5 cups chicken stock or broth
3 tablespoons chopped sage
2 cups heavy cream, whipped to stiff peaks
Salt and freshly ground white pepper

DIRECTIONS

- In a large saucepan melt 2 tablespoons of butter over low heat. Add onion and garlic. Cook until onion is translucent.
- Add butternut squash and cook for about 3 minutes. Add chicken stock and bring to a boil. Reduce heat. Add sage and simmer for 10 to 20 minutes or until tender.
- Transfer soup to a food processor or blender. Process until smooth. Strain through a fine sieve.
- Return soup to stove and finish with 2 tablespoons of butter. Whip in cream and season to taste with salt and pepper.

Serves 6.

VEGETABLES
& PASTA

Vivica's Marvelous Macaroni

INGREDIENTS

1 box elbow macaroni
2 cans cream of mushroom soup
1 cup milk
1 cup shredded cheddar cheese
Fresh black pepper
Sprinkles of Accent salt
2 eggs
½ stick butter, melted
1 capful olive oil

DIRECTIONS

· Boil noodles and then drain.
· Mix the milk and eggs together in a pot over medium heat. Bring to a slight boil and then add cream of mushroom soup and bring to a medium boil. Add salt and pepper.
· Sauté butter and oil in skillet or medium saucepan; add sauce.
· Grease casserole dish; add cooked noodles and sauce. Bake at 375°F for 30 to 45 minutes. Sprinkle with shredded cheddar cheese and then cook for 10 more minutes. Turn oven to low and cook for 10 more minutes.

Serves 6 to 8.

– JOHN ANISTON –

Greek Rice

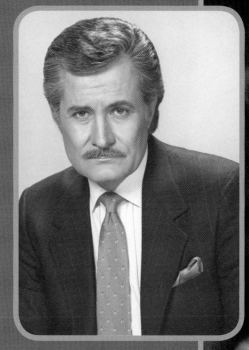

INGREDIENTS

1 ½ tablespoons olive oil
1 large onion, chopped
1 ⅓ tablespoons garlic, minced
4 cups fresh spinach, cleaned and chopped
3 tablespoons lemon juice
4 cups cooked long-grain rice
Salt and pepper to taste

DIRECTIONS

- Heat oil in a heavy pot.
- Add onion and garlic and cook on medium-high heat until onion is softened and transparent.
- Add spinach, lemon juice, and rice; cook, stirring often, until spinach is limp and rice is thoroughly heated. Add salt and pepper to taste.

Best wishes with this worthwhile cause!

LeAnn Rimes' Favorite Macaroni and Cheese

INGREDIENTS

1 12-ounce package large elbow macaroni
1 12-ounce package sharp cheddar cheese
1 12-ounce package mild cheddar cheese
1 stick butter (¼ cup)
1 pint half-and-half milk
Salt and pepper to taste

DIRECTIONS

- Heat 4 quarts of water. Add 2 teaspoons of salt. Gradually stir the elbow macaroni into the boiling water. Cook 9 to 11 minutes, stirring occasionally; do not overcook.
- Drain the macaroni; add a little salt and pepper and 1 tablespoon butter. Put half the macaroni in a Corning dish.
- Cut the sharp and mild cheeses in slices or shred and layer half on top. Then pour the rest of the macaroni on top. Layer the rest of the cheese on top of the macaroni. Cut up the remainder of the butter and place on top.
- Pour the half-and-half on top of the casserole and cover. Bake 45 minutes (more if desired) at 300°F. If you want to brown the top, you may uncover for a few minutes.

– BETTY GARRETT –

Spaghetti a la Octavia

PREPARATION

- Sauté in oil a sliced onion, green pepper, celery, and chopped garlic.
- In another larger frying pan, brown ½ pound of hamburger (we used 1 pound if we were flush). When the meat browns, stir in the sautéed vegetable mixture along with a can of Franco American spaghetti. Add a cup or more of tomato catsup, stir it all together, and heat it up.
- Serve it with Parmesan cheese, a green salad with oil and vinegar dressing, and a sliced avocado if you have a little extra change.

with love
Betty Garrett

When I first came to New York to go to the Neighborhood Playhouse, my mother and I lived in a one-room apartment with two other would-be actresses. They slept on the opened-up studio couch, and my mother and I slept in the in-a-door Murphy bed. Our kitchen consisted of a closet that opened up to a refrigerator, sink, and a two-burner hot plate.

My mother cooked for the four of us every night for a year. We had no money, so she really had to invent many inexpensive meals. Our favorite was Spaghetti a la Octavia (my mother's name). We thrived on that for a year, and to this day, when I'm by myself, I prepare this dish, and it still tastes just as good.

Stephen King

– STEPHEN KING –

Lunchtime Gloop

INGREDIENTS

2 cans Franco American spaghetti (without meatballs)

1 pound cheap, greasy hamburger

DIRECTIONS

- Brown hamburger in large skillet.
- Add Franco American spaghetti and cook till heated through. Do not drain hamburger, or it won't be properly greasy. Burn it on the pan if you want—that will only improve the flavor.
- Serve with buttered Wonder Bread.

– DONALD TRUMP –

Katerini's Lasagna

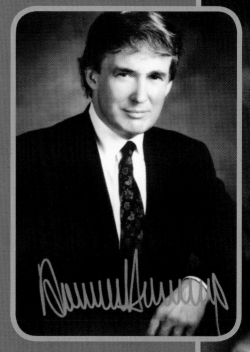

INGREDIENTS

1 pound lasagna noodles
1 to 2 pounds chopped meat
Tomato sauce
Ricotta cheese
Grated Parmesan cheese
Grated or thinly sliced mozzarella cheese (save
   some for the top)

DIRECTIONS

- Preheat oven to 350°F.
- Boil pasta till al dente. Drain in colander and let stand till cool enough to handle.
- Spread meat sauce on the bottom of the pan. Add the pasta and spread with meat sauce, ricotta, mozzarella, more meat sauce, and Parmesan cheese. Add another layer of pasta and spread with the sauce. Repeat. When complete, spread more sauce along the top and finish with the remaining mozzarella.
- Bake for 35 to 45 minutes, till bubbling.

Sauce:

- Sauté meat and drain off liquid. Add ½ cup of olive oil. Stir. Add 1 chopped onion and 3 to 4 chopped garlic cloves. Sauté until the onions are clear and tender. Add the tomato sauce and stir.
- Add salt and pepper to taste and a few bay leaves. Cook all together. Add a cup of water till the meat is tender and the sauce has thickened, about 30 to 45 minutes.
- Take out bay leaves.

Lasagna is one of my favorite dishes, and I maintain that no one prepares it better than my personal chef, Katerini.

The success you are achieving and the energy you devote to AIDS awareness is outstanding. I'm honored to be a part of this vital cause.

I'm very honored to be part of this wonderful book project.

I congratulate you for bringing such a cookbook to life and for all your support towards AIDS awareness. You have such a big heart.

Your friend, David Lewis

Enjoy!

– DAVID LEWIS –

Tettrazini for 12

INGREDIENTS

1 small turkey or 2 roasting chickens
1 large package wide noodles
4 small jars pimento
1 pound fresh mushrooms
2 cans chicken consommé
2 ½ pints heavy cream
⅓ cup dry sherry
¼ cup flour
Grated Parmesan cheese
Salt and pepper
½ teaspoon nutmeg
Paprika
1 pound small shrimp (or as many more as you prefer)

To Prepare Bird:

- Roast bird and strip carcass. Keep pieces fairly large and chunky. Save drippings of chicken fat for start of sauce.
- Sauté cut-up mushrooms in butter and set aside.

To Prepare Sauce and Noodles:

- Heat up chicken drippings and remove from heat and stir in the flour. While still off the heat, add 2 cans of consommé and mix well. Return to fire, heating it up, and stir constantly. Add sherry, salt, pepper, nutmeg, and 1 teaspoon of paprika. Stir and slowly begin to add the cream; keep stirring on fire until it reaches a cream soup consistency. Pour in buttered mushrooms and pimento. Leave on heat just long enough to blend.
- Boil noodles in water about 6 minutes and then drain. Return drained noodles to pot and add 2 cups of the sauce and toss with noodles. Have a large buttered casserole dish ready and layer the noodles, fowl, and shrimp in alternate layers. Top with remaining sauce and sprinkle generously with Parmesan cheese and paprika. Bake in a 350°F oven for about 1 hour and 15 minutes.

Nonna Rina's Zucchini Eggplant Casserole

INGREDIENTS

2 eggplants, unpeeled and cubed
3 small zucchinis, unpeeled and cubed
⅓ cup olive oil
2 large onions, thinly sliced
2 green peppers, chopped
3 tomatoes, peeled and chopped
Salt and pepper to taste
Accent seasoning and garlic to taste
1 teaspoon parsley
Pinch of grated nutmeg
½ cup grated Parmesan cheese
3 tablespoons tomato sauce
4 slices Swiss or Muenster cheese

DIRECTIONS

- Sauté onions and green peppers in oil.
- Add eggplant, zucchini, tomatoes, and tomato sauce and cook a little more until vegetables are a little soft.
- Mix in Parmesan cheese and then spread entire mixture on the bottom of a baking pan or casserole dish. Bake at 350°F for 30 minutes. Then put 4 or more slices of cheese to cover top of casserole and bake 5 or 10 minutes longer until cheese is melted.

Serves 8.

— DEBBIE REYNOLDS —

Carrot Pudding

INGREDIENTS

1 quart sliced carrots (about 6 large)
2 tablespoons finely chopped onion
2 tablespoons finely chopped green pepper
1 tablespoon salad oil or margarine
1 tablespoon flour
⅛ teaspoon sugar substitute
½ teaspoon salt substitute
1 cup skim milk

DIRECTIONS

- Cook carrots in water until tender. Drain and mash.
- Sauté onion and green pepper in oil or margarine until tender.
- Stir in flour and seasonings and cook until bubbly. Add skim milk; cook until thickened and then add carrots. Pour into lightly greased 1 ½-quart casserole and bake at 350°F for 30 minutes.

– EDDIE ALBERT –

Calabacitas Rellenas de Elote

Zucchini Squash Stuffed with Fresh Corn

You'll need a shallow ovenproof dish just large enough for the squash to fit in one layer and a blender.

6 fat zucchinis: clean and cut them into halves lengthwise and scoop out the inner flesh, leaving a shell about ½ inch thick. Discard the pulp or reserve for another use. Place the squash in the dish and set aside while you prepare the filling.

In a blender blend about 2 cups of corn, 2 medium eggs, 2 tablespoons of milk and ¼ teaspoon of salt (or to taste), to a coarse pureé. Do not add more liquid unless absolutely necessary to release the cutting blades.

6 ounces grated mild cheddar or Muenster cheese
- Mix about three quarters of the cheese into the corn purée, saving the rest for the topping.
- Fill the zucchini shells with the corn stuffing, which may be quite runny. Sprinkle with the remaining cheese.
- Place in preheated oven at 350°F. Cover the dish with foil and bake until the squash is tender, about 50 minutes. Serve covered with the tomato sauce.

This is such a colorful and attractive dish with the green squash and yellow corn topped with the tomato sauce.

Enjoy!

Salsa de Jitomate Cocida (Tomato Sauce)

You can prepare this ahead of the zucchini.

3 medium tomatoes
¼ onion, roughly chopped
1 small clove garlic, roughly chopped
2 tablespoons peanut or safflower oil
Salt to taste
- Blend the ingredients to a fairly smooth sauce. It should have some texture.
- Heat the oil, add the sauce, and cook over a medium flame for about 8 minutes until it has thickened and is well seasoned.

Good Broccoli Dish

INSTRUCTIONS

- Cook some broccoli and brown rice. Amount depends on how many people you plan on serving.
- Grate lots of cheddar cheese.
- Put broccoli and rice in a medium-sized casserole dish; distribute cheese on top. Dust with paprika. Place in hot oven for 10 to 15 minutes or under broiler. Serve with small fruit salad if you like or use salad for dessert.

I use this recipe every week though I'm not a major cook.

The cheese is chewy and good. I keep a supply of cooked rice in the fridge so I can make the dish easily after work without waiting for the rice to cook.

Greek Spinach and Rice

INGREDIENTS

2 to 3 tablespoons olive oil
1 large onion
1 package or bunch fresh spinach, washed and
drained (stems on)
1 8-ounce can tomato sauce
1 ½ cups water
½ cup (heaping) Uncle Ben's regular or brown rice
Salt and pepper to taste

DIRECTIONS

· In large pot, sauté onion in oil until soft.
· Add the remaining ingredients. Cover and cook,
  stirring occasionally. Continue simmering until
  rice is done.

This recipe becomes a "so easy to eat" side dish, but oftentimes I make a complete meal out of it! Serve it with fresh-squeezed lemon or Parmesan cheese or Louisiana hot sauce or plain. However you prefer. Enjoy!

Best wishes, Lane Brody

Sarah's Spa Supreme Tofu Vegetable Stir-Fry

INGREDIENTS

½ cup each:
   thin-sliced zucchini
   julienned carrots
   julienned red bell pepper
   julienned green bell pepper
   broccoli (break into small flowerets)
   asparagus tips
Handful of small mushrooms
½ package of extra-firm tofu (cut into cubes)
Fresh ginger, peeled, 4 thin slices (or to taste)
2 tablespoons Premier Japan Tamari sauce
2 tablespoons Sesame Seed Shake
2 tablespoons Eden Ponzu sauce
Tryson House garlic oil mist

DIRECTIONS

- Spray the garlic oil mist on nonstick skillet.
- Sauté mushrooms for a minute or so to begin to brown.
- Add cubed tofu and turn gently to brown.
- Next, add all the vegetables and sauté for 5 minutes. When partly done add the tamari sauce, sesame shake, and Ponzu sauce. Finish cooking with the cover on to steam for a minute or two. This is delicious alone or with steamed rice.

My favorite for-everyday-use recipe is a derivation of the stir-fry. It satisfies (plenty of different tastes and textures), and it can be spiced up, and it meets the critical test of "highly nutritious"!

I'm delighted to be part of this cookbook—what a worthy cause.

Best wishes, Sarah Buxton

– CHEF CHRIS SCHLESINGER –

Pasta from Hell

INGREDIENTS

2 tablespoons olive oil
1 yellow onion, diced small
1 red bell pepper, diced small
2 bananas, sliced
¼ cup pineapple juice
Juice of 3 oranges
4 tablespoons lime juice (about 2 limes)
¼ cup chopped cilantro
3 to 4 tablespoons finely chopped fresh red or
　green hot chile peppers (Scotch Bonnet or
　Habanero are best) or 4 to 6 ounces Inner Beauty
　Hot Sauce
¼ cup or so grated Parmesan cheese
2 teaspoons unsalted butter
1 pound fettuccine
Salt and freshly cracked black pepper to taste

DIRECTIONS

- In a large saucepan, heat the oil and sauté the
  onion and red pepper in it over medium heat for
  about 4 minutes.
- Add the bananas and pineapple and orange juice.
  Simmer over medium heat for 5 minutes, until
  the bananas are soft.
- Remove from the heat; add the lime juice,
  cilantro, chile peppers or Inner Beauty sauce,
  and 3 tablespoons of the Parmesan cheese and
  mix well.
- In 4 quarts of boiling salted water, cook the
  fettuccine until al dente, about 8 to 10 minutes
  for dried pasta, 3 to 4 for fresh. Drain and put
  into a stainless steel bowl.
- Add the spicy mixture, butter, and mix well.
  Season with salt and pepper to taste and garnish
  with the remaining Parmesan.

Serves 4 as an appetizer.

*Constantly challenged by my fire-eating
customers to create hotter and hotter food,
I decided to put a stop to it once and for all
by developing a dish that would satisfy their
desires and quiet their demands. A dish so
hot that there was no hotter, so hot that
never again would I have to take a ribbing
from the heat freaks.*

*This is it. Your heat source here is the
Scotch Bonnet chile pepper, widely
accepted as the hottest commercially
cultivated chile pepper in the world. Many
of my customers think this dish is just a bit
too much, Kitchen Out of Control. But
a handful of others, with sweat coming
off the tops of their heads, eyes as big as
saucers, bathed in satanic ecstasy, tell me
that it's the best thing I've ever created.
The truth lies somewhere in the middle
and in fact the heat in this dish can be
controlled by using far fewer peppers
without impairing the flavor of the dish.
But ... every once in a while, when the
really hard case sits down and insists on
something that has a real "kick" to it, I
whip the full-bore Pasta from Hell on
him. We're talking culinary respect here.*

Caramelized Crimini/ Shiitake Calzone

INGREDIENTS AND INSTRUCTIONS

- Slice 2 ounces white mushrooms into ⅛-inch slices
- Slice 2 ounces criminis into ⅛-inch slices
- Leave stem on and leave whole 8 baby shiitake mushrooms
- In 2 ounces of unsalted butter and 2 ounces of olive oil, sauté the sliced whites and criminis in a Teflon-coated pan until caramelized, about 25 minutes. Add a little water as needed so they will not burn.
- When caramelized, squeeze the juice of 1 lemon on them and 2 teaspoons of chopped fresh Italian parsley. Season with salt and pepper. Set aside and keep warm.
- Sauté the baby shiitakes in 1 tablespoon of butter with 2 cloves of fresh garlic and 1 shallot, minced. Cook for 3 or 4 minutes and then season and add them to the carmelized mixture.
- Meanwhile, roll out 6 ounces of pizza dough into a 10-inch circle. Brush surface of dough with extra-virgin olive oil. Sprinkle the oiled area with salt and pepper and 1 ounce of grated peppered Pecorino Romano.
- Meanwhile, in a bowl mix together 1 ounce of fresh goat cheese and 1 ounce of ricotta and 2 ounces of grated mozzarella, 1 teaspoon of fresh parsley, and 1 teaspoon of fresh basil.
- Place the cheese mixture just below the center of the dough in the middle and then top with the mushroom mixture. Strain any juices from the mushrooms. The calzone ingredients should be as dry as possible.
- On top of the mushrooms drizzle 1 teaspoon of white truffle oil.
- Gently fold the dough over the mushrooms and cheese and crimp the edges with a fork. On a wooden pizza peel sprinkle 1 teaspoon of fennel seeds and 2 teaspoons of cornmeal.
- Place calzone on top of cornmeal and fennel seeds. Slide the calzone into a brick-lined pizza oven (Blodgett) or equivalent at 550°F in the middle of the oven.
- Cook for 10 to 12 minutes or until golden brown.

- Remove from oven and brush immediately with extra-virgin olive oil and sprinkle with 1 ounce of grated peppered Pecorino Romano.
- Serve immediately. Only cut into calzone at the table so everyone can enjoy the perfume of the mushrooms.

Chipotle Pineapple Salsa

INGREDIENTS

½ cup crushed canned tomatoes
½ cup chipotle en adobo
1 teaspoon sea salt
2 cloves fresh garlic
¼ cup water
½ cup pineapple juice

DIRECTIONS

- Blend in a blender for 4 minutes.
- Chill for 1 hour and serve.

Fresh Mango Pineapple Salsa—Chunky Style

INGREDIENTS

¼ cup diced fresh pineapple
¼ cup diced fresh mango
¼ cup diced fresh tomato
½ teaspoon fresh grated ginger
¼ cup diced sweet onion
Juice of 1 lime
Fresh chili pepper minced to taste
¼ cup diced fresh jicama
1 tablespoon minced fresh mint
1 tablespoon minced fresh cilantro
Salt and pepper to taste

DIRECTIONS

- Mix together in bowl and serve.

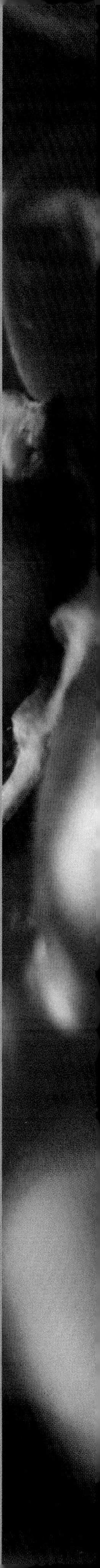

Phyllo Leeks with Sesame Crust

INGREDIENTS AND INSTRUCTIONS

Temperature: medium then low grill
or 350°F oven

- 4 leeks, split in half and washed and then blanched in boiling water
- 2 tablespoons sesame seeds
- 8 sheets phyllo dough
- 2 tablespoons bread crumbs
- 2 tablespoons olive oil
- 4 tablespoons feta cheese
- 1 egg white
- Oil spray
- Freshly ground black pepper

- Preheat oven or grill. Brush the leeks with olive oil. Lay out phyllo dough sheets one-by-one. Spray with oil spray and then sprinkle a small amount of bread crumbs between each layer. Repeat until there are 4 sheets.
- Cut the phyllo into strips the length of the leeks. Top with freshly ground black pepper. Place ½ the leeks and cheese on top and brush with egg white. Top with sesame seeds. Repeat for remaining leeks and cheese.
- Bake or grill for 25 minutes or until golden brown.

Makes 4 servings.

George Hirsch

This may taste nutty or sweet, but toasted sesame seeds offer a great crunch and a smile to a special diner in my life!

– CHEF GUY MARTIN –
Artichoke Pie

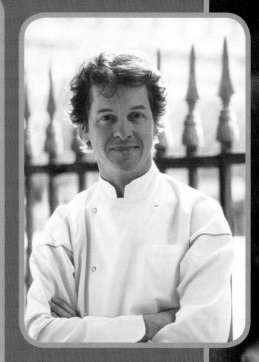

Dough:
75 grams flour
1 gram yeast
15 grams fine sugar
70 grams butter
1 egg yolk
3 grams rum

15 grams almond
  powder
1 pinch of salt
3 grams fennel
2 grams coriander

Crème Brulée:
4 egg yolks
60 grams sugar

300 grams cream
100 grams whole milk

Almond Milk Ice Cream:
125 grams almond milk
375 grams cream

125 grams whole milk
35 grams sugar

5 raw artichoke
  bottoms
5 baby carrots

1 celery stalk
250 grams fennel

Use a 29 x 22 x 6-cm dish for cooking the crème. Use
½-dome molds 3 cm wide by 2 cm deep for the fennel.

- For the dough, work the butter and then add all
  ingredients except the flour. Once it is well mixed,
  add the flour and form into a ball. Cover with
  plastic wrap and refrigerate.
- Cook the artichoke bottoms in acidified water for
  20 minutes. Dice 4 bottoms and reserve the last
  one. In a saucepan, melt 50 grams of butter with
  100 grams of sugar. Brown lightly and then add
  the diced artichokes and brown. Empty this in
  the cooking dish.
- Mix the egg yolks with the sugar and then add
  the milk and cream. Mix it all with the last diced
  artichoke bottom and pour the mixture over the
  diced artichokes. Cook in the oven at 195°F for 1
  ½ hours and then refrigerate.
- Peel the baby carrots, peel and mince the celery,
  and poach in a syrup (500 grams sugar in ½ quart
  of water) for 20 minutes.
- Chop the fennel and cook in a syrup (250 grams
  sugar in 1 cup of water) for 2 hours and then mold.
- Mix all the ingredients for the ice cream and then freeze.
- Spread the dough to a thickness of 3 mm and cut
  into 8-cm squares. Cook 5 minutes at 355°F.
- Carve the artichoke pies in 7-cm squares, caramelize
  the tops, and place each pie on a biscuit square.
- Decorate harmoniously on the serving plate.

Serves 5. (one ounce is about 28 grams, one inch is
about 2.5 cm and 1 cm equals 10 mm)

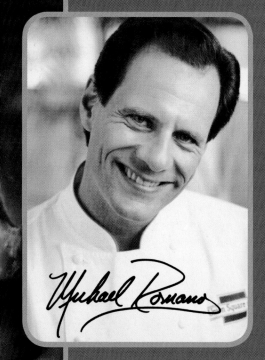

— CHEF MICHAEL ROMANO —

Malloreddus Alla Campidanese

INGREDIENTS

3 pounds canned plum tomatoes, drained (5 cups)
2 tablespoons plus 2 teaspoons olive oil
½ cup peeled and diced onion
½ cup peeled and diced carrot
½ cup diced celery
2 tablespoons minced garlic
Pinch of saffron
¼ cup chopped fresh basil
2 tablespoons chopped parsley
2 tablespoons plus 1 ¼ teaspoons kosher salt
¼ teaspoon freshly ground black pepper
¼ cup white wine
2 large tomatoes (1 pound), peeled, seeded, and diced
1 pound fresh Italian fennel sausage or sweet pork sausage and ¼ teaspoon fennel seeds
2 ounces coppa (Italian salami from pork shoulder), diced (½ cup)
Pinch of dried red pepper flakes
½ cup oven-dried tomatoes, tomato halves cut into quarters or oil-packed sun-dried tomatoes
1 cup finely grated Pecorino Romano
1 pound malloreddus or cavatelli pasta

DIRECTIONS

- Purée the drained plum tomatoes through a food mill to remove their seeds and skins. There should be 4 cups of tomato purée. Set aside.
- Heat 2 tablespoons of the olive oil in a 3-quart saucepan over medium heat. Add the onion, carrots, celery, and garlic; cook for 10 minutes, stirring occasionally to soften.
- Add the saffron, basil, and parsley to the vegetables and season with salt and pepper. Cook an additional 2 minutes. Add the white wine and

Don't be put off by the tongue-twister name of this Sardinian classic. In Sardinian dialect, malloreddus is a ridged, narrow pasta shell, often flavored with saffron. In case you can't find authentic malloreddus, substitute cavatelli. When Michael learned this recipe in the Sardinian town of Pula, he observed a technique applicable to other recipes that call for small, toothsome pasta shapes. The pasta is drained before it is even al dente, and the cooking is completed in the sauce itself, adding starchy richness in the process. Since this is an involved recipe, we've given amounts to make twice as much sauce as you will need for six appetizer servings. Freeze half to enjoy sometime when you don't feel like spending hours in the kitchen.

reduce by half over a high flame. Add the puréed tomatoes and diced fresh tomatoes, lower the flame, and simmer for 30 minutes.

- While the sauce is simmering, remove the sausage meat from its casing. Break the meat apart and sauté in a skillet with 2 teaspoons olive oil until the sausage has lost its red color but is still moist and somewhat underdone. Drain well.

- Stir in the sausage, coppa, pepper flakes, oven-dried tomatoes, and ⅔ cup of the cheese. Simmer for another 30 minutes. Stir frequently to prevent the cheese from sticking to the pan. Season with additional salt and pepper. Remove from the stove and reserve half the sauce for future use. The sauce may be prepared ahead to this point.

- Bring 4 quarts water to a boil and add 2 tablespoons salt. Cook the pasta to just before it reaches al dente and drain. Combine with half the sauce and over medium heat continue cooking the pasta until al dente. Transfer to a warm platter, sprinkle with the remaining Pecorino Romano, and serve.

Serves 6; enough sauce for 12.

This recipe is published in The Union Square Café Cookbook by Harper Collins Publishers.

Risotto Agli Asparagi (Asparagus Risotto)

INGREDIENTS

1 medium-sized onion
1 pound Carnaroli rice
5 tablespoons olive oil
1 pound fresh asparagus
1 small glass dry white wine
1 quart chicken stock
5 ounces sweet butter
2 ounces grated Parmesan cheese
1 tablespoon chopped parsley
1 garlic clove
2 ounces chopped shallots
Salt and pepper to taste

DIRECTIONS

· Chop the onion finely and cook in olive oil until translucent. Add the rice and toast for 10 seconds. Remove pan from heat and let rice toast until you are ready to cook it. Meanwhile, wash the asparagus, cut 1 inch off the bottom ends, and discard. Cut the tips of the asparagus and save them for "garnish." Place the rest of the stalks in the chicken stock and cook until very tender. Make sure the stock never boils but only simmers. Remove asparagus stalks from the stock. Purée them and place on the side. Keep the stock very hot. You will need it to cook the rice.

Risotto:

- Heat up the rice again and add the wine. Let it reduce completely. (Don't stir the rice with a spoon, but move the pan in a circular motion. This will keep the rice from sticking to the pan.) At this point start to add the broth one ladle at a time, always waiting for the stock to reduce completely. After 5 minutes, add the asparagus purée and finish cooking with the stock. When the rice is cooked, 15 to 16 minutes, remove from heat. Add the remaining butter and cheese and stir with a spoon in order to obtain a nice creamy, smooth mass, almost like the waves of the sea.

To Serve:

- Serve the rice immediately and very hot, topping it with the blanched asparagus tips.

Serves 6.

Spaghetti Aglio e Olio

INGREDIENTS

½ to ¾ cup extra-virgin olive oil, plus more for drizzling

12 garlic cloves, or more according to taste, peeled and thinly sliced

½ teaspoon red chile flakes or 2 whole cayenne peppers, or more according to taste

½ teaspoon salt

½ lemon

Large handful chopped Italian parsley

1 pound imported spaghetti

DIRECTIONS

- Heat the olive oil gently with the garlic in a small skillet. When the garlic turns opaque, add the red chile pepper flakes or whole cayenne peppers, the salt, and squeeze the lemon into the hot oil. Turn off the heat and let the garlic turn light golden at the edges. The garlic will continue to cook in the hot oil. When the oil has cooled somewhat, add the parsley.

- Meanwhile, cook the spaghetti in abundant boiling salted water until al dente. Drain the pasta well in a colander and place in a shallow serving dish. Pour the warm olive oil with the garlic, chile, and parsley over the pasta. If desired, drizzle more extra-virgin olive oil on top.

Serves 4 to 6.

Risotto al Pomodoro (Fresh Tomato Risotto)

INGREDIENTS

¼ cup extra-virgin olive oil
½ onion, peeled and finely chopped
4 garlic cloves, peeled and minced
¼ cup red wine
8 Roma tomatoes, peeled, seeded, and chopped
10 to 12 fresh basil leaves, chopped
2 cups arborio rice
6 to 7 cups water or chicken broth, or a mixture of both
Salt and freshly ground black pepper to taste
2 tablespoons unsalted butter
¾ cup grated Parmesan cheese

DIRECTIONS

- Heat the olive oil in a heavy 2-quart saucepan. Add the onion and cook over low heat until it is tender. Add the garlic and when it gives off its characteristic aroma, add the wine and the tomatoes. Cook over moderate heat until the tomatoes break down and form a sauce. Add the rice, turn the heat to low, and cook slowly until the rice absorbs all the tomato sauce.
- Meanwhile, heat the water or broth until it is very hot. Turn off the heat but keep the liquid hot on a warm burner. Add the hot liquid to the rice over low heat. Wait until all the liquid is absorbed before adding the next ladle of broth. Midway in the cooking time, add salt and pepper to taste.
- When the risotto is just tender, add the butter and Parmesan cheese. Turn off the heat and stir risotto vigorously until all the butter and cheese are absorbed.

Variations: Fresh mozzarella, pesto

Serves 4 to 6.

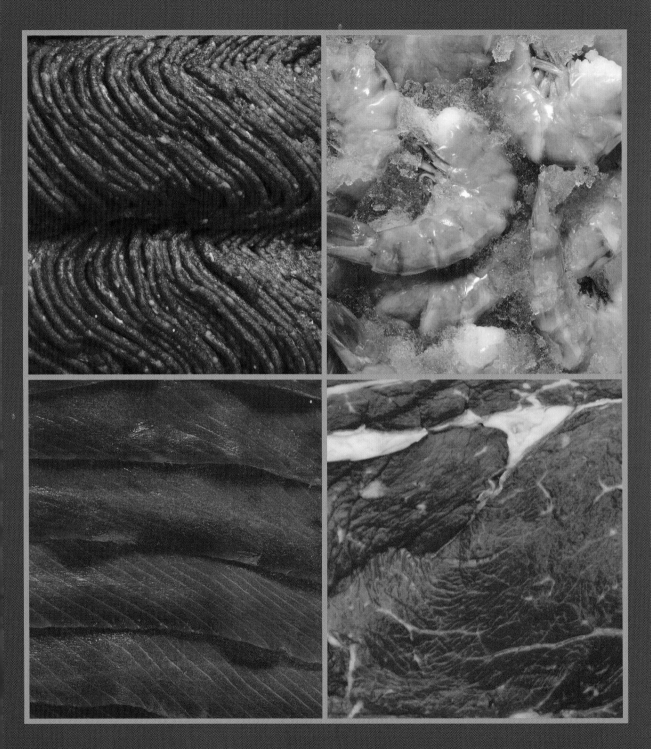

MEATS, POULTRY,
& FISH

Great Meatloaf

INGREDIENTS

1 ½ to 2 pounds hamburger meat (or ground turkey)
1 can tomato sauce
1 package of McCormick meatloaf seasoning
1 egg
Bread crumbs

DIRECTIONS

· Mix all ingredients together.
· Bake 1 to 1 ½ hours at 350°F or until done.

Note: Reserve ½ can tomato sauce to pour on top of meatloaf before baking.

We are glad to help in any way we can with this cookbook. It sounds like an exciting project. Here is one of Faith's favorite recipes. Enjoy!

Randy Brown, Faith's Friend

faith hill

– SIEGFRIED & ROY –

Pichelsteiner

INGREDIENTS

1 pound sirloin tip roast, lean, ¾-inch cubes
1 pound veal, lean, ¾-inch cubes
1 pound lamb, lean, ¾-inch cubes
1 pound pork, lean, ¾-inch cubes
3 large potatoes, peeled, sliced into ⅛-inch lengths
2 medium onions, peeled, sliced into ⅛-inch lengths
½ pound carrots, peeled, sliced into 1/16-inch lengths
½ pound green beans, cut into 1-inch lengths
3 parsnips, each cut ¼-inch thick
1 bunch parsley, chopped
2 medium leeks, cut lengthwise, ⅛-inch crosswise
1 celery root, chopped roughly
2 medium rutabaga or turnips, cut into 1-inch cubes
4 bacon strips (lard may be substituted)
1 ½ quarts beef stock
Salt and freshly ground pepper
Paprika
Caraway seeds
Parsley sprigs, for garnish

Many greetings from Las Vegas and from Siegfried & Roy!

Pichelsteiner is one of the most favorite traditional German Eintopf (one-pot dinners) for healthy appetites. Serve with German black rye bread, butter, and beer.

DIRECTIONS

- Add sliced onions, paprika, caraway seeds and mix together with the cubed meat and set aside.
- Peel, chop, or slice all vegetables as directed and separate into individual piles.
- Grease bottom of large stew pot with lard or bacon. Place the meat and seasoning mixture in the bottom of the pot. Add salt and pepper. Cook over medium heat for 15 minutes. **Do not cover the pot.**
- Place in the pot each individual pile of vegetables in layers. Season each layer with a small amount of salt and pepper. The top layer must be potatoes only. Add cold beef stock and cover pot. Bring to a slow boil and cook for up to 90 minutes until meat is tender. Do not lift cover off pot or stir or you will end up with mush.
- Divide the Pichelsteiner into plastic containers, garnish, cover, and place in freezer.

Martha Stewart

Turkey 101
Perfect Roast Turkey

If your roasting pan only fits sideways in the oven, turn the pan every hour so the turkey cooks and browns evenly.

INGREDIENTS

20 to 21-pound fresh whole turkey (giblets and neck removed from cavity and reserved)
1 ½ cups unsalted butter (3 sticks), melted, plus 4 tablespoons unsalted butter at room temperature
1 bottle dry white wine
1 teaspoon salt
2 teaspoons freshly ground pepper
Classic Stuffing (see recipe below)
1 cup dry red or white wine for gravy (optional)
Giblet Stock (see recipe below)

DIRECTIONS

- Rinse turkey with cool water and dry with paper towels. Let stand for 2 hours at room temperature.
- Place rack on lowest level in oven. Heat oven to 450°F. Combine melted butter and white wine in a bowl. Fold a large piece of cheesecloth into quarters and cut it into a 17-inch, 4-layer square. Immerse cheesecloth in the butter and wine; let soak.
- Place turkey, breast side up, on a roasting rack in a heavy metal roasting pan. If the turkey comes with a pop-up timer, remove it; an instant-read thermometer is a much more accurate indication of doneness. Fold wing tips under turkey. Sprinkle ½ teaspoon salt and pepper inside turkey. Fill large cavity and neck cavity loosely with as much stuffing as they hold comfortably; do not pack tightly. (Cook remaining stuffing in a buttered baking dish for 45 minutes at 375°F.) Tie legs together loosely with kitchen string (a bow will be easy to untie later). Fold neck flap under and secure with toothpicks. Rub turkey with the softened butter and sprinkle with remaining 1 ½ teaspoons salt and pepper.

- Lift cheesecloth out of liquid and squeeze it slightly, leaving it very damp. Spread it evenly over the breast and about halfway down the sides of the turkey; it can cover some of the leg area. Place turkey, legs first, in oven. Cook for 30 minutes. Using a pastry brush, baste cheesecloth and exposed parts of turkey with butter and wine. Reduce oven temperature to 350°F and continue to cook for 2 ½ more hours, basting every 30 minutes and watching pan juices; if the pan gets too full, spoon out juices, reserving them for gravy.
- After this third hour of cooking, carefully remove and discard cheesecloth. Turn roasting pan so that the breast is facing the back of the oven. Baste turkey with pan juices. If there are not enough juices, continue to use the butter and wine. The skin gets fragile as it browns, so baste carefully. Cook 1 more hour, basting after 30 minutes.
- After this fourth hour of cooking, insert an instant-read thermometer into the thickest part of the thigh. Do not poke into a bone. The temperature should reach 180°F (stuffing should be between 140° and 160°F), and the turkey should be golden brown. The breast does not need to be checked for temperature. If legs are not yet fully cooked, baste turkey, return to oven, and cook another 20 to 30 minutes.
- When fully cooked, transfer turkey to a serving platter and let rest for about 30 minutes. Meanwhile, make the gravy. Pour all the pan juices into a measuring cup. Let stand until grease rises to the surface, about 10 minutes, and then skim it off. Meanwhile, place roasting pan over medium-high heat. Add 1 cup dry red or white wine, or water, to the pan. Using a wooden spoon, scrape the pan until liquid boils and all the crisp bits are unstuck from pan. Add giblet stock to pan. Stir well and bring back to a boil. Cook until liquid has reduced by half, about 10 minutes. Add the defatted pan juices and cook over medium-high heat 10 minutes more. You will have about 2 ½ cups of gravy. Season to taste, strain into a warm gravy boat, and serve with turkey.

Serves 12 to 14.

Classic Stuffing

The terms "stuffing" and "dressing" are often used interchangeably, but they do have different meanings: stuffing is cooked inside the bird, dressing on its own.

INGREDIENTS

12 tablespoons unsalted butter

4 onions (2 pounds), peeled and cut into ¼-inch dice

16 celery stalks, cut into ¼-inch dice

10 large fresh sage leaves, chopped, or 2 teaspoons crushed dried sage

6 cups homemade or low-sodium canned chicken stock

2 loaves stale white bread (about 36 slices), crust on, cut into 1-inch cubes

2 teaspoons salt

4 teaspoons freshly ground pepper

3 cups coarsely chopped flat-leaf parsley leaves (about 2 bunches)

2 cups pecans, toasted and chopped (optional)

2 cups dried cherries (optional)

DIRECTIONS

- Melt butter in a large skillet. Add onions and celery and cook over medium heat until onions are translucent, about 10 minutes. Add sage, stir to combine, and cook 3 to 4 minutes. Add ½ cup stock and stir well. Cook for about 5 minutes, until liquid has reduced by half.

- Transfer onion mixture to a large mixing bowl. Add all remaining ingredients, including the remaining stock; mix to combine.

Makes 12 cups.

Giblet Stock

The giblets are edible when properly prepared and are the secret to a fine broth and gravy. Make this while the turkey roasts.

INGREDIENTS

Giblets (heart, gizzard, and liver) and neck reserved from turkey
4 tablespoons unsalted butter
1 onion, peeled and cut into ¼-inch dice
1 celery stalk with leaves, stalk cut into ¼-inch dice, leaves roughly chopped
1 small leek, trimmed, washed, and cut into ¼-inch dice
Salt and freshly ground pepper
1 bay leaf

DIRECTIONS

- Trim any fat or membrane from giblets. The liver should not have the gallbladder, a small green sac, attached. If it is, trim it off carefully, removing part of the liver if necessary. Do not pierce the sac; the liquid it contains is very bitter. Rinse giblets and neck and pat dry.
- In a medium saucepan, melt 3 tablespoons butter over medium heat. Add chopped onion, celery and leaves, and leeks. Cook, stirring occasionally, until onions are translucent, about 10 minutes. Add ½ teaspoon salt and ¼ teaspoon pepper and cook another 5 minutes. Add 4 cups water, bay leaf, gizzard, heart, and neck (do not add liver; it needs to be cooked separately, or it makes the stock bitter). Bring to a boil and then reduce to a high simmer. Cook for 45 minutes or until gizzard is tender when pierced with the tip of a knife.
- Meanwhile, chop the liver finely. Melt remaining tablespoon of butter in a small skillet over medium-low heat. Add liver and cook, stirring constantly, 4 to 6 minutes, until liver no longer releases any blood and is fully cooked. Set aside.
- After the 45 minutes of simmering, the liquid should reduce to about 2 ½ cups. If it has not, increase the heat and cook another 10 to 15 minutes.
- Strain broth. Chop gizzard and heart very fine and add to strained broth along with chopped liver. Pick meat off neck and add to broth. Set aside until needed for gravy.

Makes about 2 cups.

I wish you much success with this project!

Newman's Own Marinated Steak

INGREDIENTS

½ cup Newman's Own Olive Oil and Vinegar
Dressing
2 cloves garlic, crushed
1 large onion, cut up
Salt and pepper
1 large sirloin steak, about 1 ½ inches thick

DIRECTIONS

· Combine Newman's Own, garlic, onion,
and dash of salt and pepper in a shallow glass
dish. Add steak; turn to coat with marinade.
Refrigerate several hours, turning steak
occasionally.
· Just before serving, preheat broiler or grill.
Drain steak and broil or grill. Slice and serve.

Makes about 4 servings.

Veal Paprikash

INGREDIENTS

2 pounds veal shoulder
2 tablespoons shortening
1 large onion, chopped
1 clove garlic
1 green pepper, chopped
1 fresh tomato, chopped
Salt, pepper, paprika to taste
1 cup water
Green pepper rings for garnish

DIRECTIONS

· Cut the meat into 1-inch cubes. Sauté in the shortening over low heat with the chopped onion, garlic, and green pepper for 5 minutes. Add the tomato and the seasonings and then stir in the 1 cup water. Cover and continue cooking gently until the meat is tender, about 1 hour. If you want more gravy, add a little more water as it cooks. Serve garnished with green pepper rings.

This recipe is courtesy of the book Cooking with Love and Paprika *by Joseph Pasternak.*

– CHEF JIM SHIEBLER –

Roasted Sea Bass with Lemon Zest Crust

Five Spice Whipped New Potatoes, Chinese Longbeans, Citrus Segments and Grilled Cantaloupe, Avocado, Tarragon Compote©

INGREDIENTS

4 8-ounce portions sea bass filets
1 tablespoon lemon peel, yellow portion only, minced
1 pound new potatoes
4 garlic cloves, peeled and head removed
1 teaspoon Chinese five spice powder
1 tablespoon nonfat yogurt
¾ pound Chinese longbeans, clean and cut into 3 inch pieces
1 pint pink grapefruit, peeled and segmented
1 orange, peeled and segmented
1 lime, peeled and segmented
1 lemon, peeled and segmented
1 ripe avocado
½ cantaloupe, peeled, seeded and sliced
1 shallot, minced
1 teaspoon Bertolli Extra Virgin olive oil
1 teaspoon fresh tarragon, chopped cracked black pepper to taste

DIRECTIONS

- Potatoes: In a sauce pan, add potatoes, garlic and five spice. Fill with water until above the level of potatoes by approximately 2 inches. Boil potatoes. When potatoes are fully cooked, drain off the excess water. Whip with a fork and add yogurt and cracked pepper.
- Sea Bass: Press lemon zest into the sea bass filets. Season with cracked pepper. Sear in a nonstick Teflon pan until golden brown on the outside. Place in a 350°F pre-heated oven and bake until just under done. (Time depends on the thickness of the fish. A 1-inch thick filet will take approximately 7-8 minutes). At this time, steam the longbeans.
- Compote: While potatoes are boiling and fish is roasting, grill cantaloupe until semi soft. Peel, pit and dice the avocado. Dice the cantaloupe and mix with avocado, shallots, olive oil, and tarragon. Season with cracked pepper and set aside.
- To Plate: Spoon whipped potatoes in the center of the plates. Top with longbeans and top with roasted sea bass. Surround with citrus segments and top fish with grilled cantaloupe, avocado, tarragon compote. Enjoy.

Yield: 4 Portions

Larry's Chili

DIRECTIONS

- Begin with "Carroll Shelby's Three Alarm Chili."
- Substitute turkey breast for the ground beef.
- Substitute beer for the water.

Bill Blass' Meatloaf Recipe

INGREDIENTS

2 pounds chopped sirloin with ½ pound veal and
  ½ pound pork (grind all together)
1 cup chopped celery
1 cup chopped onions
½ cup parsley
⅓ cup sour cream
1 ½ cups bread crumbs (soft)
1 egg beaten with 1 tablespoon Worcestershire sauce
Bottle Heinz chili sauce
3 strips bacon
Salt and pepper to taste
Pinch of thyme and marjoram

DIRECTIONS

· Preheat oven to 350°F.
· Sauté celery and onions in butter. Add
  remaining ingredients and form a loaf.
· Top with chili sauce and bacon strips. Cook 1
  hour.

Serves 6.

– SHIRLEY MACLAINE –

Gourmet Lamb Stew

INGREDIENTS

1 leg of lamb, weighing
5 to 6 pounds
1 tablespoon lard or
shortening
2 tablespoons flour
1 clove garlic, peeled
and minced
About 3 cups water
2 tablespoons tomato
paste
¼ teaspoon bouquet
garni
1 teaspoon salt
⅛ teaspoon freshly
ground black pepper

10 sugar cubes
1 tablespoon water
1 teaspoon beef extract
1 small yellow onion,
peeled
6 pearl onions, peeled
2 small yellow turnips,
peeled
2 small carrots, scraped
3 tablespoons sweet
butter
1 teaspoon sugar
1 tablespoon chopped
fresh parsley

Best wishes!
Shirley MacLaine

DIRECTIONS

· Have butcher prepare lamb as follows: remove
fell and bone, trim off excess fat, cut lamb into
1 ½-inch cubes.

· Heat lard or shortening in large skillet until
sizzling; add lamb and brown on all sides until
golden, stirring. Sprinkle flour over meat; cook a
few minutes, stirring constantly. Add garlic; cook
over very low heat until garlic begins to smell.
Add water (enough to barely cover meat), tomato
paste, bouquet garni, salt, and pepper. Cover;
simmer about 15 minutes.

· Meanwhile, put sugar lumps and 1 tablespoon of
water in small saucepan; heat over low heat until
sugar caramelizes. Add to meat; stir to blend well.
Cover; simmer 45 minutes, stirring occasionally.

· Prepare vegetables as follows: chop yellow onion,
leave pearl onions whole, chop turnips into large
pieces, and dice carrots.

· Heat butter in large skillet until hot; add
vegetables, sprinkling with 1 teaspoon of sugar.
Cook over low heat until golden, stirring
occasionally. Add vegetables to lamb, cover, and
simmer 50 minutes or until vegetables and meat
are fork-tender, stirring often.

· Remove vegetables and meat to heated platter.
Skim off surface fat before pouring sauce over the
meat. Garnish with chopped parsley. Serve with
crusty French bread and tossed crisp green salad.

Serves 6 to 8.

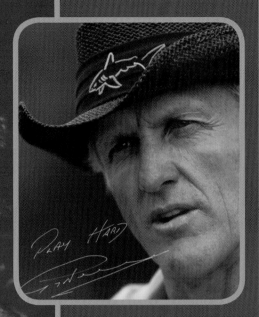

Australian Meat Pie

INGREDIENTS

1 ounce butter or margarine
2 small onions, finely chopped
2 pounds chopped sirloin
2 tablespoons plain flour
2 ½ cups beef bouillon or stock
Salt and pepper to taste
1 teaspoon dried thyme
2 tablespoons Worcestershire sauce
¼ cup chopped parsley
Pinch of nutmeg
Pastry (store-bought pastry dough works very well)
1 egg, slightly beaten

DIRECTIONS

- Melt butter in a saucepan. Add onions and fry over moderate heat until onions soften.
- Add beef and fry, pressing down with fork until beef is browned; drain.
- Sprinkle flour over beef, stir, and continue cooking for a further 2 minutes. Remove pan from heat and gradually add stock.
- Return pan to the heat and stir constantly until mixture boils and thickens.
- Add all remaining ingredients. Cover pan and simmer over a low heat for 30 minutes.
- Line pie tin with pastry. Prick the base several times with a fork. Using a sharp knife, trim off excess pastry. Spoon filling in. Brush around edge with beaten egg. Top with pastry, pressing edges together. Cut a hole in center of pie. Brush with remaining egg.
- Cook at 400°F for 25 minutes or until crust is golden brown.

Serves 4 or 5.

Fire and Ice Chili a la Rogers

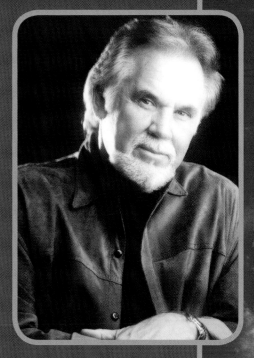

INGREDIENTS

1 20-ounce can pineapple chunks in syrup
1 28-ounce can whole tomatoes, with juice
1 6-ounce can tomato paste
1 4-ounce can diced green chilies
3 cloves garlic, pressed or minced
2 medium-sized yellow onions, chopped
1 green bell pepper, seeded and chopped
¼ cup chili powder
4 teaspoons ground cumin
1 tablespoon diced jalapeño chilies (for more fire,
    add 2 tablespoons jalapeño chilies)
2 teaspoons salt
2 tablespoons olive oil
2 pounds lean boneless pork butt, cut into
    1-inch cubes

Condiments:
Small bowls of sliced green onions, shredded
    cheddar cheese, and dairy sour cream

I'm pleased to share one of my very favorite recipes with you. You have to taste my "Fire and Ice Chili" to believe how delicious it is. This is chili to warm a Southern boy's heart and soul.

DIRECTIONS

· Drain pineapple, reserving syrup. Drain and
  chop tomatoes, reserving juice. In large bowl,
  combine reserved syrup, tomatoes and juice,
  tomato paste, green chilies, 2 cloves garlic,
  1 onion, bell pepper, chili powder, cumin,
  jalapeño chilies, and salt.
· Heat olive oil in Dutch oven until very hot.
  Brown pork on all sides in batches. (Don't
  overcrowd pot. Add just enough pork to cover
  bottom.) With all browned pork in pot, add
  remaining garlic and onion. Cook until onion is
  soft. Add tomato mixture to pork mixture. Cover
  and simmer 3 hours, stirring occasionally.
· Add pineapple for the last 30 minutes of cooking.
  Serve with condiments.

Serves 8 to 10.

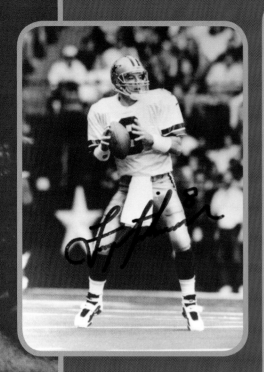

Troy's Favorite Meatloaf

INGREDIENTS

1 ½ pounds ground beef

1 egg, beaten

2 tablespoons chopped green pepper

1 small onion, chopped

1 tablespoon basil

Seasoned salt and pepper to taste

Seasoned bread crumbs (from a stuffing mix), about 1 cup

Equal portions of barbeque sauce and milk to moisten crumbs (about ¾ cup total, depends upon amount of stuffing used)

½ cup each of cheddar and Monterey Jack cheeses, shredded

DIRECTIONS

· Pour liquid over crumbs to moisten; set aside.

· Mix rest of ingredients (except cheeses); add bread mixture. Adjust more or fewer crumbs to your own preference and add more barbeque sauce, if needed, to keep meatloaf moist.

· Pat meat into a ½-inch-thick rectangle on a square of tin foil or waxed paper. Sprinkle cheeses all over meat (to within 1 inch of edges). Roll up jellyroll fashion and pinch all around to seal.

· Put seam side down in pan. Bake at 350°F about 1 ½ hours or until done.

Pedernales River Chili

INGREDIENTS

4 pounds chili meat (coarsely ground round steak
   or well-trimmed chuck. If specially ground, ask
   butcher to use ¾-inch plate for coarse grind)
1 large onion, chopped
2 cloves garlic
1 teaspoon ground oregano
1 teaspoon comino seed
6 teaspoons chili powder (or more if needed)
1 ½ cups canned whole tomatoes
2 to 6 generous dashes liquid hot sauce
Salt to taste
2 cups hot water

DIRECTIONS

· Place meat, onion, and garlic in large heavy fry
  pan or Dutch oven. Cook until light colored.
  Add oregano, comino seed, chili powder,
  tomatoes, hot sauce, salt, and hot water. Bring to
  boil, lower heat, and simmer about 1 hour. Skim
  off fat during cooking.

Lady Bird Johnson

*Over the years, I have come
to collect and treasure a
number of recipes that reflect
Texas' heritage, and I'm
delighted to share my recipe
for "Pedernales River Chili,"
attesting to the Spanish and
Mexican influence on Texas
cuisine. It was served in the
"Texas White House"!*

*Best wishes and "Cheers!" for
your efforts towards AIDS.*

Donatella Versace

Warm regards!

Duck a l'Orange

INGREDIENTS

2 ducks
Vegetable broth
2 glasses of freshly squeezed orange juice
2 oranges to garnish
2 spoons of Cointreau
1 spoon of olive oil
1 teaspoon vinegar
1 teaspoon sugar
1 bunch of sage
1 bunch of rosemary

DIRECTIONS

- Carefully clean the ducks and salt inside and outside and then put them on pan with a spoon of olive oil and let them brown all over, turning them often. The heat under the pan should be moderate. Pour the Cointreau over the ducks and let it dry off. Then add sage and rosemary. Cover the pan with a lid and cook the ducks for 1 hour and 30 minutes (approximately), adding vegetable broth little by little if the ducks dry out too much. Before the ducks are completely cooked, add the orange juice (now the heat under the pan must be high) and let the juice dry a bit. Dissolve the sugar in the vinegar and pour into the juice.
- Skim the fat from the sauce, cut the ducks in pieces, taking out the parts of bones, and place them in a baking pan, pour the sauce over, cover, and keep in a warm oven.
- Cut the oranges, keeping the skin, in round slices, stir them in a pan (1 minute per side), and use them to garnish the ducks. Ducks can be served with mashed carrots.

Serves 6.

– HUGH FULLER –

White Relleno
A Belizean/Yucatecan
Mayan Dish

INGREDIENTS

½ teaspoon cumin
1 teaspoon black pepper
1 teaspoon thyme
½ teaspoon cloves
1 teaspoon garlic powder
½ teaspoon cinnamon powder
1 teaspoon oregano
Salt to taste
1–12 lb turkey
2 pounds ground pork
2 tablespoons olive oil
1 teaspoon saffron
5 heads garlic
2 cups raw pearl onions
1 medium size onion
5 whole roasted poblano chile peppers
1 cup golden raisins
1–6 ounce bottle pitted green olives
½ –6 ounce bottle capers
1 dozen eggs
1 cup white wine
Flour to thicken
White corn tortillas

DIRECTIONS

- Boil nine eggs until hard.
- Remove egg yolk from whites and chop all whites, putting whole yolks aside.
- Season pork with about half of the first ingredients and pan fry lightly with 2 tablespoons of olive oil.

Originally from Belize, where he was one of that country's premier broadcasters, both as a music personality and a newscaster, Hugh Fuller brings his own unique and distinctive style to 94.7 The Wave in Los Angeles.

A graduate of the University of San Francisco, Hugh worked in the San Francisco area on local television and radio stations hosting weekly specials and as reporter/anchor/talk show host for many years.

An accomplished pianist, he also worked as an actor and has voiced countless commercials and industrials. He is a regular host on PBS, KCET–TV's pledge drives.

- When pork is cooked lightly (not over done), mix in: chopped onion, all the chopped egg whites, half of the olives (chopped), all the capers, half of the raisins, three whole raw eggs to bind the ingredients.
- Stuff turkey alternately with seasoned pork and nine whole egg yolks beginning and ending with the pork. Secure the stuffing by passing several trussing pins through the skin on both sides of the main cavity. Secure the drumsticks with linen kitchen string.
- Combine the rest of the first eight ingredients plus the saffron in enough water to simmer the stuffed turkey.
- Lay turkey flat in a roaster on top of the stove.
- Add seasoned water (as much as the roaster will hold) and simmer on medium heat/basting periodically, until turkey is done (instant read thermometer plunged into the thickest part of the thigh should register 175° F).
- While turkey is simmering, on a grill, roast the heads of garlic (not totally peeled), poblano peppers and peeled pearl onions.
- When turkey is done remove from water, brown quickly (for presentation only), in 400° F oven.
- Thicken water that the turkey was in slightly with flour. End result should be light soup. Once lightly thickened, add roasted onions, peppers, and garlic, the rest of the capers, whole olives, raisins, and white wine to taste.
- Carve turkey.
- Add turkey, pork stuffing, and soup to a bowl and eat with warm corn tortillas.
- Enjoy!

Hugh Fuller credits his friend Mrs. Patricia Vernon of the Hospital Auxiliary in Belize for this wonderful recipe – which has become his favorite!

– JOHN TRAVOLTA –

Crab Quiche

INGREDIENTS

Pie Crust:
½ cup chilled butter
3 tablespoons vegetable shortening
2 cups all-purpose flour
5 to 6 tablespoons cold water
½ teaspoon salt

Filling:
1 pound jumbo lump cleaned crabmeat (fresh, not frozen)
2 tablespoons chopped fresh tarragon
2 tablespoons chopped fresh basil
1 tablespoon chopped fresh chervil
1 cup grated Jack cheese
1 ½ cups grated Gruyere cheese

Custard:
1 ½ cups heavy cream
3 eggs and 1 yolk
Salt and pepper to taste

DIRECTIONS

- Preheat oven to 350°F.

Pie Crust Dough:

- Put chilled butter and shortening in mixer with the flour and salt. Use paddle attachment. Mix on medium speed until blended, 3 to 4 minutes (it will look like cornmeal) and then add the water. As soon as dough comes together, turn off mixer. This should take only about 10 seconds. (Do not overmix!) Take out of machine and chill in refrigerator for about 1 hour.

Custard Filling:

- Mix all custard ingredients.
- Roll out dough to about ¼ inch thick.
- Line bottom of 9-inch pie dish.
- Sprinkle ½ of each cheese on bottom.
- Add crabmeat.
- Sprinkle on the herbs.
- Sprinkle on the rest of cheese.
- Pour custard over all the ingredients almost to the top of pie dish.
- Cook for 1 hour and 15 minutes.
- Let stand for 30 minutes before serving.

Polly Bergen's Chili

INGREDIENTS

6 large onions, finely chopped
6 large green peppers, finely chopped
3 cloves garlic, minced
Cooking oil
6 pounds ground round or chuck
5 16-ounce cans Italian-style tomatoes
4 to 6 16-ounce cans kidney beans (drained)
2 6-ounce cans tomato paste
Salt and pepper to taste
2 teaspoons wine vinegar
5 whole cloves
3 bay leaves
4 tablespoons chili powder, or more to taste
4 drops Tabasco sauce, or to taste
Sugar
2 teaspoons cumin

DIRECTIONS

- In a large roaster, sauté garlic in oil and remove. Sauté onions and peppers until golden; remove and drain. Add meat to oil, separate with a fork, and cook until all meat is gray in color. Drain off accumulated oil.

- Add onions and green peppers to the meat, mix well, and then add all of the remaining ingredients. Cover and simmer over low heat for 1 hour. Simmer uncovered for another hour. Remove cloves and bay leaves before serving.

Makes 25 servings.

New Mexico Grilled Tuna Steaks with Garlic and Pepper

DIRECTIONS

- Marinate: mahi or other tuna steaks in diluted lime juice for 15 to 30 minutes.
- Fire: your coals (mesquite preferred). When the coals are hot, your grill is ready.
- Baste: tuna steaks with mixture of olive oil, garlic purée, and powdered deep red New Mexican pepper. Never measure your ingredients; always guess!
- Grill: tuna steaks over hot coals. Leave on first side until top of steaks start to sweat with juice and then turn only once.
- Eat: with green steamed vegetables, Matanzas Creek chardonnay, and friends.

Daniel McVicar

This is my favorite summer grill stolen from my favorite chefs—enjoy!

This is a tasty combination of a burrito and a taco … A "baraco" as my son and daughter say. The last time I went backpacking with my son, I prepared this backcountry meal that attracted the attention of a mama bear and her two cubs. With some pot banging, they figured out that there wasn't enough for them, but I thanked them for their attention and considered it a compliment.

– DANIEL MCVICAR –

Dan's Bear Baiting Baracos

BRING WITH YOU

- 1 pound ground beef
- 2 red, green, or yellow peppers
- Serrano chilis

Hide in Your Son's Backpack Prior to the Hike Up the Mountain:
- 1 Guinness beer

USE YOUR SWISS ARMY KNIFE TO

- Dice any peppers you have brought, green, yellow, and red. 1 or 2 is good.
- Dice 2 serrano chilis, removing the hot ribbing and seeds inside.

Take 1 pound of beef:
- Brown in pot and drain off excess fat in fire—be careful!
- Stir in peppers.
- Add splash of the Guinness beer that your son brought up the mountain without his knowledge.
- Serve on tortillas, roll 'em up, and hand 'em out.

Mmm … tasty; watch out for the bears.

– JOSH TAYLOR –

Pot Roast

INGREDIENTS

4 pounds round bone roast
1 cup chili sauce
1 large onion, sliced
2 stalks celery with leaves
1 12-ounce can beer
8 medium baking potatoes, cut into quarters
8 carrots, cut into 2-inch pieces
2 tablespoons dried parsley flakes

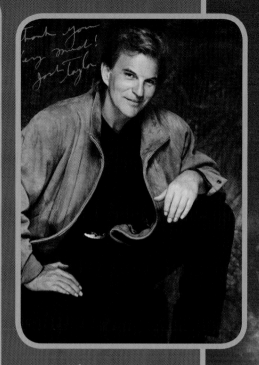

DIRECTIONS

- Preheat oven to 325°F.
- Place roast in roasting pan. Top with chili sauce, onions, and whole celery stalks. Bake uncovered for 1 hour. Pour beer over and cover. Bake for 1 ½ hours.
- Place potatoes and carrots around roast. Cover and bake 1 hour more until the vegetables are fork tender. Remove celery stalks.
- Degrease gravy and add parsley.
- Arrange roast and vegetables on platter and serve gravy separately.

Serves 8.

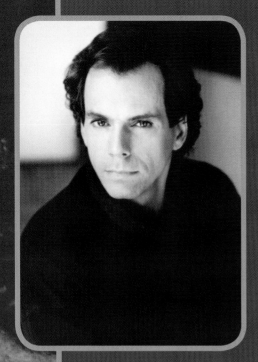

Raymond O'Neill's Rabbit Stew with Beer

INGREDIENTS

1 3 ½- to 4-pound rabbit, cut into serving pieces
4 tablespoons butter
2 tablespoons olive oil
18 pearl onions, peeled
6 ounces bacon, cut into bite-sized pieces
4 tablespoons flour
1 bottle beer
1 cup chicken stock
1 teaspoon tarragon
¼ cup fresh parsley, chopped
2 cloves
1 teaspoon black pepper, freshly ground
½ teaspoon liquid "maggi" sauce (available at most grocery stores)
2 tablespoons commercial liverwurst (coarse or fine, preferably with herbs)
Fresh ground sea salt to taste

DIRECTIONS

- Heat butter and olive oil in a large skillet. Add the onions and the bacon and cook until golden. Remove the onions and bacon and reserve.
- Dust the rabbit pieces with flour seasoned with salt and pepper and fry them on both sides in the bacon fat/butter/oil until brown.
- Add the beer and chicken stock and then stir in the cloves, pepper, and tarragon and the "maggi" sauce. Add the onions and the bacon and cover. Simmer for 1 hour.
- Ladle out a ½ cup of the stew juices and mix in the liverwurst (to liquefy it) and then add it to the stew. Simmer for 10 more minutes. Season with sea salt to taste. Serve this stew over couscous, rice, or mashed potatoes, sprinkled on top with the chopped parsley.

Raymond O'Neill

This is a recipe for rabbit stew that I make with beer because it's different and delicious. Stews are one of those "comfort" foods that most people like, and the recipe can be easily prepared with chicken or turkey if rabbit is hard to get. Enjoy!

*Rabbit is higher in protein and lower in saturated fat, sodium, and calories than beef, lamb, pork, chicken, or fish.

– DAVID BALDACCI –

Shore Lunch

INGREDIENTS

4 filets of fish, chicken, or turkey

1 cup bread crumbs

1 cup Rice Krispies (powderized with rolling pin
before measuring)

1 cup flour

½ cup potato pearls or buds (not instant powder)

½ cup parsley

2 tablespoons seasoned salt

Egg wash: 2 eggs, 2 tablespoons milk; whip until
blended

DIRECTIONS

- Blend all dry ingredients together.
- Dip choice of each filet in egg wash and then coat
  filet completely with breading.
- Fry over medium heat in butter or Crisco oil.
  (Fish filets: 3 minutes per side; chicken or turkey
  filets: 5 minutes per side.)
- Enjoy!

Serves 4.

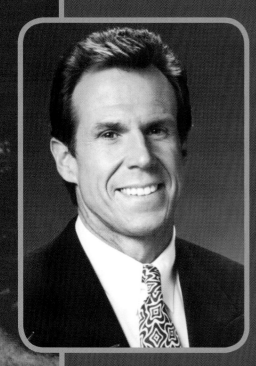

Bill Boggs [signature]

Hello from "Bill Boggs Corner Table"

Turkey Loaf

INGREDIENTS

1 ½ pounds ground lean turkey
½ cup Italian bread crumbs
1 egg
¾ cup salsa
¼ cup chopped fresh parsley

DIRECTIONS

- Combine bread crumbs, egg, and salsa and add to ground turkey. Mix well and add fresh chopped parsley.
- Place in a loaf pan and spoon more salsa on top. Bake at 350°F for 1 hour.

Serves 4 or 5.

Spare Ribs, Chicken, Loin of Pork, or Baked Ham Marinade

DIRECTIONS

- Put 2 rib slabs in a pot of boiling water (to cover) and simmer about 3 to 5 minutes.
- Take rib slabs out of water and put in pan to marinate. Let cool.

Marinade:

2 ½ cups brown sugar

2 cups bourbon

¾ cup soy sauce

2 tablespoons cornstarch

4 cloves fresh grated or crushed garlic

1 teaspoon grated fresh ginger

⅛ cup cider vinegar

3 teaspoons Worcestershire sauce

1 teaspoon dry mustard

- Mix all marinade ingredients and dissolve sugar thoroughly, making a kind of thick sauce.

To Cook:

- Salt and pepper ribs or chicken, pork, or ham. If rack is available, put ribs on rack in pan to cook in.
- Pour marinade over ribs or other meats and marinate overnight if possible or as long as your time allows. Baste frequently.
- Start oven at 500°F for 20 minutes and then reduce to 300°F. Baste frequently while cooking, turning ribs once in a while. Ribs should be finished cooking in about 1 ½ hours.

If any of the above meats are going to be barbequed, it takes about the same amount of time to cook as in the oven, 1 ½ hours.

Turkey Spaghetti Sauce

INGREDIENTS

1 package lean ground turkey meat
1 jar favorite red pasta sauce
1 white onion, chopped
1 red bell pepper, chopped
2 small yellow squash, chopped
1 small zucchini squash, chopped
4 mushrooms, chopped

DIRECTIONS

- Cook meat thoroughly, drain, add vegetables, cook approximately 5 minutes, add sauce, and simmer 5 minutes.
- Serve over your favorite pasta and top with grated cheese.

This is one of our family recipes we make often at our house. We are always looking for ways to substitute turkey or chicken for meat.

It's quick and easy, and the leftovers are yummy!

I think this cookbook is a great idea, and I wish you much success. Bon appétit!

Jacklyn Zeman

– ROGER CLINTON –

Roger's Meat Marinade and Basting Sauce

INGREDIENTS

½ cup barbeque sauce (Preferably McClard's from Hot Springs, Arkansas … the best in the world)

¼ cup Italian dressing (low or nonfat)

¼ cup ranch dressing

¼ cup grated Parmesan cheese

2 tablespoons mustard

2 tablespoons A1 Steak Sauce

2 tablespoons ground black pepper

1 tablespoon Lawry's seasoned salt

1 teaspoon garlic powder

1 teaspoon lemon pepper

½ teaspoon Tabasco sauce

DIRECTIONS

· Stir all ingredients vigorously!

· Marinate choice of meat in sauce for 2 hours and grill accordingly. Baste while grilling.

This book is a very worthy cause, and it's an honor to be included.

Enjoy!

AIDS awareness is very important, and I wish you tremendous success with your wonderful project. It's truly amazing what a few individuals can do when they come together as a group.

Congratulations on a wonderful project!

*This recipe was inspired by Diane Clement in her book More Chef on the Run.

– DIANA KRALL –

West Coast Clams

INGREDIENTS

3 pounds fresh West Coast clams
1 or 2 cloves garlic, crushed
1 large shallot or 3 tablespoons green onion, chopped
¼ to ½ cup butter
1 14-ounce can Italian tomatoes, with the juice
1 cup dry white wine
½ cup canned clam nectar or water or wine
Salt and pepper to taste
¼ cup fresh basil
Dash hot crushed chili peppers (optional)
Fresh parsley for garnish (optional)

DIRECTIONS

- Melt butter in a large shallow pan. Sauté garlic and shallot or onion in butter. Cover and simmer gently for just a few minutes so as not to burn garlic.
- Add the tomatoes plus their juice, white wine, clam nectar, water or more wine, spices, salt, and pepper. Bring to a gentle boil.
- Add clams and reduce the heat to low until the shells open, about 6 to 8 minutes. Discard any shells that do not open.
- To serve, place several clams in each serving bowl and ladle the juice on top. Sprinkle with fresh parsley and serve with plenty of fresh bread to sop up the juices.

– TOMMY TUNE –

The Secret Remoulade Sauce

INGREDIENTS

2 cups mayonnaise

3 green onions with tops, finely chopped

1 tablespoon parsley, finely chopped

3 hard-cooked eggs, finely chopped

2 tablespoons Zatarain's mustard or other Creole mustard

2 stalks celery off of stock, finely chopped

2 tablespoons red wine vinegar

1 tablespoon cooking sherry wine

1 tablespoon paprika

Salt and pepper to taste

A little sugar to taste

DIRECTIONS

· Combine all ingredients and mix until well blended. Make at least one day in advance. Serve with shrimp or crabmeat.

Makes 1 quart.

This remoulade sauce has been a secret in the Tune family for years. It comes from one of my late mother's church friends, Audrey Albert. It's delish!

Thank you for writing this book and also for asking for my participation. It is a fine thing you are doing. All my best, Tommy Tune

MEAT, POULTRY, & FISH

Chicken and Dressing Casserole

INGREDIENTS

4 pounds chicken
2 teaspoons salt
2 peeled onions
4 stalks celery, sliced
1 carrot, sliced
1 can cream of chicken soup
1 can cream of celery soup
¼ cup cooking sherry
12 ounces evaporated milk
8 ounces seasoned bread crumbs
¼ cup melted butter
1 cup slivered almonds

DIRECTIONS

- Cook chicken in a large pot with the salt, onions, celery, and carrot. When done, remove the meat from the bone; tear chicken into small pieces (reserve 1 cup of basting).
- Purée vegetables in a food processor along with cup of basting.
- In a saucepan heat soups, sherry, and evaporated milk. Mix with vegetable purée.
- In a bowl mix bread crumbs and butter.
- To build casserole, pour 1 cup of the soup mixture in the bottom of a large casserole dish, topping with half of the stuffing and then half of the chicken. Repeat and finish by topping with the almonds. Bake in a 325°F oven for 30 to 40 minutes.

Makes 8 servings.

– GLORIA GAYNOR –

Gloria Gaynor's Chicken Dish

INGREDIENTS

8 chicken parts (breasts and/or thighs)
1 10-ounce can condensed cream of chicken soup
1 3-ounce can B in B sliced mushrooms
4 ounces sour cream
4 ounces whole milk
2 ounces cooking sherry

DIRECTIONS

- Season chicken parts lightly with Lawry's seasoned salt (or any seasoned salt), garlic powder, and pepper. Bake chicken in oven at 425°F for 40 minutes.
- While chicken cooks, pour soup into a saucepan and slowly stir in sherry, sour cream, milk, and mushrooms, in that order. Keep stirring until the mixture is smooth and hot.
- When the chicken is brown, pour the soup mixture over all pieces and return the chicken to the oven for an additional 15 minutes. Serve with yellow rice and steamed carrots and broccoli.

* I promise happy guests and rave reviews.

I'm sure you've heard the expression, "Necessity is the mother of invention." Well, the following is a recipe I created one evening out of necessity.

During a meeting in his office one evening, my husband called to tell me we would be having company for dinner. He said they would be leaving the office in about half and hour. My first thought was to tell him to stop by Kentucky Fried Chicken or some other fast food place on the way home. Then I realized that he probably thought it would pose no problem for me. I came from a large family and always cooked a large dinner. As our office was only half an hour from our home, I had to make a dinner that would be quick, delicious, and impressive. Those are things men rarely think about. Using just what I had on hand, this is what I came up with.

Enjoy!

MEAT, POULTRY,
& FISH

83

Enjoy!

Chicken Parisienne

INGREDIENTS

6 chicken breasts (boneless)
1 can cream of mushroom soup
1 8-ounce carton sour cream
1 can (3 or 4 ounces) mushrooms, undrained
4 tablespoons dry white wine
½ cup fine dry bread crumbs
Parmesan cheese
Paprika

DIRECTIONS

- Remove skin on chicken breasts and salt with pepper on both sides. Arrange chicken in single layer in buttered shallow dish.
- Combine soup, sour cream, mushrooms, and wine and pour over chicken. Sprinkle with bread crumbs, Parmesan cheese, and paprika. Bake uncovered 45 to 60 minutes at 375°F. Can be made ahead and refrigerated.

Green Chile Chicken Enchilada Casserole

INGREDIENTS

2 10 ½-ounce cans cream of chicken soup
1 10 ½-ounce can cream of mushroom soup
3 4-ounce cans chopped green chilies
12 ounces grated cheddar cheese
12 corn tortillas, fresh
3 large chicken breasts
Pepper
Splash of milk

DIRECTIONS

· Bake the chicken breasts at 350°F for approximately 45 minutes to 1 hour, until cooked through. Cool and shred chicken by pulling apart with forks.

· In a medium saucepan, stir together cans of soup and chiles over low heat until warm. Add a splash of milk.

· Spread a couple tablespoons of the soup/chile mixture on the bottom of a rectangular medium-sized baking dish and then cover completely with tortilla pieces (torn in quarters or smaller).

· Begin layering in the following manner: soup mixture, chicken, cheese, and tortillas. Repeat once or twice, depending on the depth of baking dish; top with cheese. Bake at 350°F until bubbly, approximately 45 minutes. Let cool 5 minutes and then serve.

This is an easy favorite to serve to groups. The recipe can be doubled. Serve alone or with a dollop of sour cream and a side of beans or crispy tortilla chips.

Enjoy!

Chicken and Rice

INSTRUCTIONS

- Brown chicken pieces (white and/or dark) in frying pan with olive oil and garlic. When brown, place in roasting pan; cover with 1 can of mushroom soup.
- In a separate casserole dish, mix together 1 cup of rice, 1 can of consommé, and 1 can of water. Bake both dishes for 1 hour at 325°F.

It is an honor to be included in this special book for a great cause.

My "Chicken and Rice" has been a family recipe that never fails.

Wishing you great success in your endeavors.

– ELIZABETH TAYLOR –

Elizabeth Taylor's Chicken with Avocado and Mushrooms

INGREDIENTS

1 small avocado (preferably the dark-skinned California variety)
1 tablespoon lemon juice
2 small chickens (2 ½ pounds each), cut into serving pieces
Salt and freshly ground pepper
¼ cup butter
3 finely chopped shallots
3 tablespoons cognac
⅓ cup dry white wine
1 cup heavy cream
2 cups sliced fresh mushrooms
1 cup chicken stock
Chopped parsley for garnish

DIRECTIONS

- Peel and cube avocado; sprinkle with lemon juice. Cover and refrigerate.
- Sprinkle chicken with salt and pepper.
- In a large heavy skillet, over low heat, heat 3 to 4 tablespoons butter and sauté chicken until juices run yellow when pricked with a fork, about 35 to 40 minutes (use two skillets if necessary, adding more butter as needed).
- Transfer cooked chicken to a serving dish. Cover loosely with aluminum foil. Keep warm in a 300°F oven for 15 minutes while preparing sauce.
- Add shallots to skillet. Cook over medium heat, stirring and scraping sides and bottom of pan with a wooden spoon. Add cognac and wine and bring to a boil. Boil until mixture has almost evaporated. Add cream and boil 5 minutes longer.
- In a saucepan over high heat, sauté mushrooms in 3 tablespoons of butter.
- Add chicken stock to cream mixture. Cook over medium heat, stirring constantly, until thick. Add the mushrooms and avocado cubes. Stir until well blended. Pour over warm chicken. Sprinkle with parsley.

Serves 6 to 8.

Curry Chicken Vindaloo

Preparation time: 1 ½ hours
Cooking time: 45 minutes

INGREDIENTS

2 pounds chicken, cut in pieces
½ cup mustard oil
4 bay leaves
1 large onion, thinly sliced
1 teaspoon salt
10 cloves garlic, crushed
1 tablespoon thinly sliced root ginger or powder
1 medium tomato, peeled and quartered
1 ¼ cups water

Spices:
1 teaspoon green cardamom seeds
2 teaspoons turmeric powder
1 teaspoon paprika pepper

Paste:
3 tablespoons vindaloo powder
2 teaspoons vinegar
2 teaspoons salt

DIRECTIONS

- First combine the paste ingredients to make a smooth mixture. Make a few deep gashes on the chicken pieces and rub the paste over them. Leave to marinate for 1 hour.
- Heat the mustard oil in a saucepan over a moderate heat. Add the bay leaves and cardamom seeds, stir, and then add the onion and fry until light brown. Then add the remaining spices, stir well, and add the chicken pieces. Continue to cook, stirring for about 5 minutes. Add the salt, garlic, ginger, and tomatoes and cook for a further 10 minutes, still stirring.
- When the fat starts separating, add water. Stir once or twice. Cover with a tight-fitting lid, lower the heat, and leave to simmer for about 25 minutes until the chicken is tender. Serve hot.

Serves 6.

Jay Leno's Uncle Louie's Chicken Wings Marinara

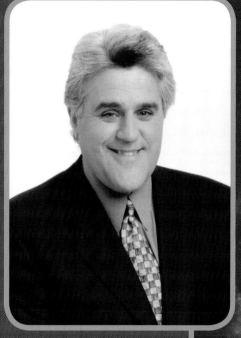

INGREDIENTS

2 to 3 dozen chicken wings
1 can Italian whole plum tomatoes
Olive oil
Garlic or garlic powder
Durkee's hot sauce
Salt
Fresh parsley, chopped

DIRECTIONS

- Cook chicken wings by broiling or lightly flour them and deep fry in safflower or peanut oil. While they are cooking, prepare the sauce.
- Heat ⅛ inch of olive oil in a pan; add garlic powder or crushed garlic to taste. Mash one can of whole plum tomatoes through a sieve and cook in the olive oil. Add a few teaspoons of chopped parsley and salt to taste and then cook about 20 minutes. At the end of this cooking time, add Durkee's hot sauce (put in a little or a lot, depending on how hot or mild your taste), but put in at least 2 tablespoons, or the sauce won't be as tasty. Add a little garlic powder and cook another 3 to 4 minutes.
- In a bowl, toss the chicken wings with ½ cup of the sauce and serve with the remaining sauce on the side to dip the wings into.

Enjoy!

Bob Hope's Favorite Chicken Hash

INGREDIENTS

2 chicken breasts (broiled)
2 strips bacon (crisp)
½ small onion (sauté)
2 tablespoons butter
½ teaspoon lemon juice
2 tablespoons sour cream
1 tablespoon dry sherry wine
Salt and pepper

DIRECTIONS

- Cut chicken in fine strips.
- Crumble crisp bacon and combine with the sautéed onion, butter, lemon juice, salt, and pepper. Sauté until thoroughly heated in the butter and add chicken strips.
- Shortly before serving, add sherry and sour cream. Do not allow to cook after adding the sherry and sour cream. Just heat through.

— BARBARA TAYLOR BRADFORD —

Chicken in the Pot

INGREDIENTS

6 chicken legs

6 cans College Inn chicken soup or four to six large
    chicken bouillon cubes dissolved in two pints water

6 large carrots cut into 1-inch pieces

6 parsnips cut into 1-inch pieces

1 large onion, left whole

12 potatoes (medium sized), peeled and cut in half

Herbs:

8 bay leaves

1 teaspoon herbs of Provence

4 tablespoons dried parsley (or same amount of
    fresh parsley, finely chopped)

Pepper to taste

Pinch or two of grated nutmeg

DIRECTIONS

· This dish is cooked on top of stove for
approximately 1 hour. Place chicken legs in
a large pot and cover with chicken soup or
bouillon. Reserve remainder of soup to use later,
if required.

· Add all the herbs, the carrots, the chopped
parsley, the large whole onion, and bring to a boil.
Once pot is boiling, lower heat to medium. Stir
chicken and leave to simmer for half an hour.

· For last half hour of cooking time, add potatoes
and parsnips. If necessary, add remainder of
chicken soup. Ingredients in pot should be
covered at all times so they remain moist and
succulent. Serve chicken, vegetables, and soup in
large soup bowls.

Serves 6.

Douglas Fairbanks Jr.'s Chicken Casserole

INGREDIENTS

White bread, crusts removed, soaked in milk
Cooked chicken, cut in pieces (preferably breasts)
Onion, chopped or cut in rings
Ham (preferably smoked), sliced
Half-and-half (or whole milk or cream)
Butter
Salt and pepper

DIRECTIONS

- Preheat oven to 350°F. Line a Pyrex-type casserole dish with milk-soaked bread. Lay in alternate layers of cooked chicken pieces, a little bit of the onion, a slice of ham, another layer of milk-soaked bread, more chicken and ham, and so forth, until dish is full.
- Add half-and-half, or milk or full cream if you want it richer, dot with butter, add salt and pepper to taste, and bake in oven until thoroughly heated through. If you want the top crusty, heat under broiler for a few seconds.

This can be made ahead, refrigerated, and then heated later.

President Bill Clinton's Favorite Recipe: Chicken Enchiladas

Bill Clinton

INGREDIENTS

Cooking oil
2 4-ounce cans chopped green chilies
1 large clove garlic, minced
1 28-ounce can tomatoes
2 cups chopped onion
2 teaspoons salt
½ teaspoon oregano
3 cups shredded, cooked chicken
2 cups dairy sour cream
2 cups grated cheddar cheese
15 corn or flour tortillas

DIRECTIONS

- Preheat oil in skillet. Sauté chopped chilies with minced garlic in oil.
- Drain and break up tomatoes; reserve ½ cup liquid. To chilies and garlic, add tomatoes, onion, 1 teaspoon salt, oregano, and reserved tomato liquid. Simmer uncovered until thick, about 30 minutes. Remove from skillet and set aside.
- Combine chicken with sour cream, grated cheese, and other teaspoon salt.
- Heat ⅓ cup oil; dip tortillas in oil until they become limp. Drain well on paper towels.
- Fill tortillas with chicken mixture; roll up and arrange side by side, seam down, in 9 x 13 x 2-inch baking dish. Pour tomato mixture over enchiladas and bake at 250°F until heated through, about 20 minutes.

Yields 15 enchiladas.

"Chicken and Chestnuts in Lettuce Cups" is a light but deliciously delectable Oriental recipe that I greatly enjoy.

I give you my best wishes and every success for this book, which is a wonderful idea for a deserving cause.

Paloma Picasso's Favorite Recipe: Chicken and Chestnuts in Lettuce Cups

INGREDIENTS

500 grams minced chicken (or turkey)
5 dried Chinese mushrooms
1 red pepper, finely chopped
2 cloves garlic, crushed and chopped
2 stalks lemon grass, finely chopped
½ inch ginger, finely chopped
1 bunch spring onion, sliced
1 230-gram can bamboo shoots, finely chopped
1 230-gram can water chestnuts, finely chopped
2 tablespoons sunflower oil
1 tablespoon sesame oil
1 tablespoon soy sauce
1 tablespoon oyster sauce
1 tablespoon dry sherry
1 teaspoon sambal oelek (Indonesian chili spice)
½ cup water
1 head iceberg lettuce
2 tablespoon coriander

DIRECTIONS

- Soak dried mushrooms in hot water for 30 minutes.
- Drain and rinse bamboo shoots and water chestnuts and chop finely.
- Drain the mushrooms and finely chop.
- Heat 1 tablespoon of sunflower oil in a wok, add the minced chicken in batches until brown, and remove and set aside.
- Heat the remaining 1 tablespoon of sunflower oil and sesame oil in wok and add garlic, ginger, and lemon grass and stir-fry for one minute; add the red pepper, chicken, mushrooms, bamboo shoots, water chestnuts, spring onion, sauces, sherry, water, and sambel oelek and stir-fry until everything is mixed and piping hot. Sprinkle in the coriander.
- Separate lettuce leaves, forming a cup, and scoop the stir-fried chicken into the lettuce cups and serve.

Serves 4.

Chicken Zehme

INGREDIENTS/DIRECTIONS

- Rinse 1 7-pound roasting chicken inside and out and pat dry.
- Cut 1 orange in quarters and squeeze juice over chicken inside and out.
- Salt chicken cavity and stuff with orange rind and 1 small onion, quartered.
- Tie chicken legs together with kitchen string.
- Sprinkle bird all over with salt and pepper and then sprinkle 1 teaspoon dried rosemary and 1 teaspoon dried thyme over it.
- Place chicken in roasting pan, breast up, and pour ½ cup of white wine over chicken. Bake at 400°F for 20 minutes. Then reduce heat to 350°F for an additional 1 hour and 30 to 40 minutes (depending on oven) until golden brown.
- Prepare glaze while chicken is roasting. Spoon glaze over chicken after approximately 1 hour of cooking.

Glaze:

- Heat 3 tablespoons each of unsalted butter, Dijon mustard, honey, and 1 tablespoon of apricot jam until hot.
- Remove from heat and stir in 3 tablespoons orange liqueur.

Enjoy!

Chaz's Chicken Crisp

INGREDIENTS/DIRECTIONS

With whatever amount of chicken desired:

- Put about ¾ inches of vegetable oil in a medium-sized pot.
- Clean and cut up chicken (lightly rinse under water and dry with paper towel).
- Lightly season chicken pieces in this order: seasoning salt, garlic salt, ground pepper, and onion salt.
- Beat 2 eggs and lightly dip each piece of chicken in beaten egg.
- Dip each piece into all-purpose flour (shake well-well-well in the flour); this will make chicken crispier than normal.
- Test oil by sprinkling a pinch of flour in oil. When the flour sizzles, the oil is ready. Put chicken pieces in batches in the pot and cook at least 20 to 25 minutes or until done. Pierce chicken with a knife and if chicken is red or runny, it's not done!

Nancy O'Dell's Chicken Casserole

INGREDIENTS

2 cups diced cooked chicken

1 cup cooked rice

1 tablespoon chopped onion

1 can mushroom soup

1 can water chestnuts, sliced and drained

¾ cup Hellman's mayo

1 package frozen French-style beans, cooked 5 minutes, or 1 can French-style beans

3 chopped hard-boiled eggs

DIRECTIONS

- Mix all ingredients and top with following: melt one stick margarine and mix with one roll Ritz crackers, crushed for topping.
- Refrigerate casserole several hours or overnight. Bake 30 minutes at 350°F.

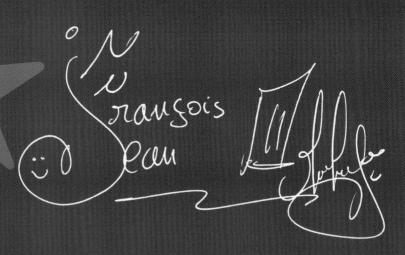

— CHEF JEAN FRANCOIS METEIGNER —

Lobster Ravioli with Lobster Ginger Sauce

Filling

INGREDIENTS

- 9 ounces salmon filet with no skin, no bones, and no fat
- 3 egg whites
- 1 teaspoon chopped ginger
- 1 teaspoon chopped garlic
- ⅓ cup cream (use lobster sauce if you don't want cream or oil)
- 3 live lobsters
- ½ cup chives

DIRECTIONS

- Boil lobsters for four minutes, remove meat, and put aside. Retain shells for sauce. In food processor, turn salmon and egg whites for one minute. Add salt, pepper, and ginger; turn. Add cream in small amounts.
- Cut lobster into medium-sized pieces and mix into salmon mousse. Add chives.

Note: Do not overmix the mousse in food processor.

Sauce
INGREDIENTS

Lobster shells
1 onion, diced
1 carrot, diced
2 stalks celery
3 tablespoons tomato purée
2 cloves garlic, peeled and diced
2 sprigs rosemary
2 sprigs thyme
1 ounce fresh ginger

DIRECTIONS

- Cut lobster carcasses into medium-sized pieces. Sauté in very hot olive oil for 5 minutes. Add onion, carrot, celery, garlic, and tomato purée to pan and sauté. Add herbs. Cover with water and cook for 30 minutes. Strain, pressing lobster shells to get all juice out. Reduce for 10 minutes and set aside.
- Mix ginger and lobster sauce in blender for 1 minute. Strain and put aside.
- To make ravioli, fill wonton skins with mousse; shape into a ½ moon. Poach and serve topped with sauce.

*Café Portofino owner
Giuseppe Avocadi*

– CAFÉ PORTOFINO –

Chicken Angelo

INGREDIENTS

1 pound boneless, skinless chicken breasts
1 cup quartered artichoke hearts
¾ cup flour
½ cup white wine
2 tablespoons chopped garlic
⅛ cup olive oil
½ cup chicken broth
8 ounces linguine, cooked al dente
Chopped parsley
Salt and pepper to taste

DIRECTIONS

• Heat olive oil in sauté pan on medium heat. Cut chicken into one inch cubes and sprinkle with salt and pepper. Lightly coat chicken with flour and sauté until golden brown. Add garlic to chicken during the last minute of sautéing. Add white wine and artichoke hearts. Cook until wine is reduced by a third. Add chicken broth, butter, and parsley. Cook until chicken is tender. Toss with cooked linguine and garnish with chopped parsley.

Serves 4 people.

Fricassee of Chicken with Tarragon Vinegar

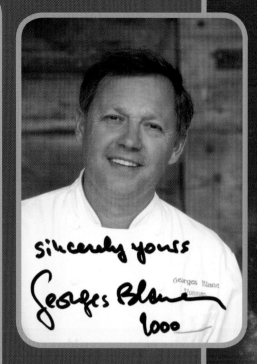

INGREDIENTS

4 pounds frying chicken
½ pound butter
12 small onions
5 shallots
3 fresh tarragon branches
3 unpeeled garlic cloves
3 roughly cut-up carrots
3 ⅓ ounces tarragon wine vinegar
7 ounces consommé
1 tablespoon concentrated tomato paste
1 tablespoon flour
1 teaspoon mustard
1 pint double cream
½ cup crushed strained tomatoes

DIRECTIONS

- Cut the chicken in 8 pieces (2 thighs, 2 legs, 2 breasts, and 2 wings); place in a heavy pan with a generous piece of butter on high heat to brown lightly and evenly. Add the carcass cut in 3 pieces. Salt and pepper to taste.
- Add the carrots, the shallots, the onions, and garlic; cover and cook in a hot oven.
- Halfway through cooking (about 20 minutes), wet with a thin stream of vinegar so that the steam that is produced thoroughly penetrates the meat.
- When the chicken is cooked, make the sauce by removing the chicken pieces and placing them in another container. Degrease the pot; add a little more vinegar and then the consommé. Reduce the mixture and then add the combined mustard, flour, and tomato paste. Add the double cream and reduce until you get a nice consistency. Pass the sauce through a "chinois"; add the crushed tomatoes and the minced tarragon. Check and adjust the seasoning if necessary.
- Place on a serving platter and accompany with Creole rice or pilaf and seasonal vegetables for garnish.

Serves 4 people.

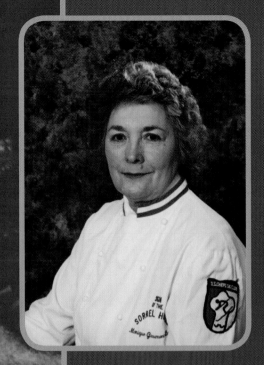

Monique Gaumont-Lanvin

Pheasant Casserole in Burgundy Wine

INGREDIENTS

One 2 ½- to 3-pound pheasant
½ teaspoon ground rosemary
¼ teaspoon curry powder
¼ teaspoon ground juniper
Salt and pepper
½ chopped onion
2 tablespoons clarified butter or olive oil
2 ounces flour
2 tablespoons tomato paste
1 pint burgundy wine
Pheasant Stock:
1 onion
1 carrot
Bay leaf
Pinch of thyme

DIRECTIONS

- Joint the pheasant: first remove the legs and then cut away the two breast sections, down and along the backbone. Cut the two leg sections in half at the joint and cut each breast in two. Trim off the wing section. Place all the bone sections in a pot with one onion and one carrot, roughly chopped; add thyme, bay leaf, and a little salt. Cook for about 1 hour at a slow simmer. Strain and reserve stock.
- Mix the seasonings together and sprinkle on the pheasant pieces. Sauté quickly in hot clarified butter till brown on all sides. Add the flour, browning slightly and then the tomato paste, stirring while adding the wine and some of the reserved stock to just cover the pheasant. Cook at a slow simmer for 45 minutes to 1 hour.
- If desired, add 2 ounces of fresh chanterelle mushrooms, a splash of heavy cream, or fresh cranberries.

Serves 4.

Michael W. Beary

Grilled Chilean Sea Bass over Basmati Rice with Roasted Red Bell Pepper / Artichoke Vinaigrette

INGREDIENTS/DIRECTIONS

2 7-ounce Chilean sea bass filets
Basmati Rice:
1 cup rice
2 cups water
1 tablespoon butter
Pinch salt and pepper
Pinch lemon zest

- Boil water, butter, salt, pepper, and lemon zest. Pour over rice in ovenproof dish, cover tightly, and bake at 350°F for 20 to 30 minutes. When finished, toss with fork and cover again until served.

Roasted Red Bell Pepper / Artichoke Vinaigrette:
1 large red bell pepper
2 artichokes
2 large red beefsteak tomatoes, juice only
2 lemons, juice and small amount of zest only
1 shallot, chopped fine
Pinch salt and pepper

- Roast bell pepper on a hot grill until skin is burnt. Remove skin and discard. Julienne the flesh of the pepper and set aside. Cook artichokes and dice hearts into ⅛-inch cubes; julienne the edible part of the inner leaves and save a few outer leaves for garnish.
- Sauté shallots in 2 teaspoons of extra-virgin olive oil for 30 seconds on medium heat, add tomato juice, and simmer briefly for 1 minute. Add peppers and artichokes, warm gently, and finally add salt, pepper, and enough lemon juice to be flavorful but not too acidic. Keep warm.

FINAL PREPARATION

- Lightly coat sea bass filets with canola oil, salt, and pepper. Grill on a well-oiled grill at a medium-hot temperature until the filet excretes a milky juice. Place filet over the rice, add a liberal amount of vinaigrette, and garnish with artichoke leaves and vegetables of your choice. Bon appétit!

Serves 2.

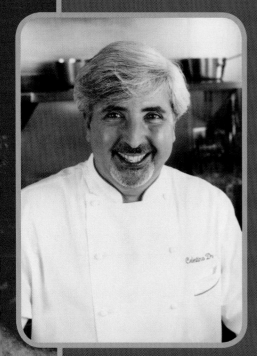

Risotto Nero

INGREDIENTS

12 ounces arborio rice
1 tablespoon chopped shallots
2 cloves chopped garlic
4 tablespoons olive oil
2 tablespoons chopped Italian parsley
4 ounces squid, clean and cut
4 ounces shrimp, cut in half
4 ounces bay scallops
1 cup white wine
2 envelopes squid ink
Chicken or vegetable broth

DIRECTIONS

- In a saucepan, add oil, shallots, and garlic. Place pan on medium flame. When shallots begin to turn color, add rice and stir for 2 to 3 minutes. Add wine, let evaporate, and start to add broth little by little.
- Add seafood, squid ink, salt, and pepper. Keep adding broth using a wooden spoon and mix until risotto is ready (about 25 minutes).
- Remove from fire, add parsley, and serve.

– CHEF BOB BEAUDRY –

Pecan-Crusted Softshell Crabs with Corn Bread and Cabbage Slaw

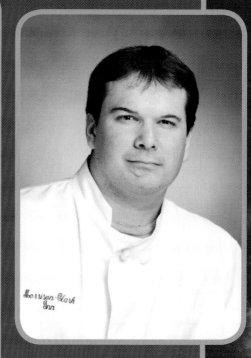

Corn Bread:

½ cup white wine
1 ½ teaspoons salt
6 tablespoons soft butter
2 eggs
1 cup cornmeal

1 ¾ cups all-purpose flour
2 ½ teaspoons baking powder
1 ½ cups heavy cream

- Preheat oven to 375°F. Lightly grease a 10-inch square pan.
- In a bowl, cream the sugar, salt, and butter; mix in eggs one at a time.
- In separate bowl mix the flour, baking powder, and cornmeal together.
- In three additions add the dry mixture and heavy cream, starting and ending with the dry.
- Bake in greased pan until golden brown.

Cabbage Slaw:

¼ cup apple wood smoked bacon, sliced
½ cup grilled corn, cut off cob
¼ cup diced poblano pepper
4 cups shredded savoy cabbage, slightly blanched

¼ cup chopped pecans
2 cups heavy cream
¼ cup chives, finely diced
Salt and cayenne pepper, to taste

- Cook bacon slowly over low heat until crisp.
- Add the next 5 ingredients and cook until cream has thickened slightly.
- Add the chives, salt, and cayenne.
- Serve over the warm corn bread with the softshell crab leaned against its side.

Softshell Crab:

4 softshell crabs, cleaned
1 cup buttermilk
¾ cup ground pecans
¼ cup flour

1 tablespoon salt
1 teaspoon pepper
¾ cup peanut oil

- Soak cleaned crabs in buttermilk for 10 minutes.
- Meanwhile, mix together the pecans, flour, salt, and pepper.
- Preheat the oil to 360°F in a large sauté pan.
- Slightly drain crabs and coat completely in pecan mixture.
- Carefully place top side down into heated oil and brown completely, flip over and brown bottom, drain on towel, and serve with corn bread and slaw.

Crisp Dungeness Crab Cake with Grilled Citrus and Watercress Salad, Meyer Lemon Balsamic Dressing

Crab Cake

INGREDIENTS

2 cups or approximately 10 ounces freshly cooked Dungeness crab meat

½ cup fresh white bread crumbs, dried in oven

2 teaspoons lemon juice

1 tablespoon pasilla, minced

1 tablespoon sweet red bell pepper, minced

1 tablespoon sweet yellow bell pepper, minced

1 tablespoon red onion, minced

1 tablespoon celery, minced

1 tablespoon Italian parsley, chopped

¼ cup mayonnaise

¼ teaspoon kosher salt

1 teaspoon freshly cracked pepper

Pinch of cayenne

DIRECTIONS

· In bowl, combine all the ingredients. Taste and adjust seasonings if necessary.

· Form the crab mixture into 8 cakes. Heat a Teflon skillet or griddle to 325 to 350°F with just enough oil or butter to coat the bottom. Fry the crab cakes until they are golden brown on each side and heated through, approximately 3 minutes per side. Serve with grilled citrus and watercress salad and top with Meyer lemon balsamic dressing.

Grilled Citrus and Watercress Salad

INGREDIENTS

1½ cups fresh-squeezed tangerine juice

½ cup Meyer lemon juice

½ cup balsamic vinegar

2 tangerines, peeled and sliced into ½-inch-thick slices

2 Meyer lemons, peeled and sliced into ½-inch-thick circles

½ cup watercress sprigs

1 handful baby frisee

1 handful mizuna

Kosher salt

Freshly ground black pepper

Olive oil

DIRECTIONS

- Meyer Lemon Balsamic Dressing: Combine the tangerine juice, Meyer lemon juice, and balsamic vinegar into a non corrosive saucepan. Place over high heat and reduce until it coats the back of a spoon. Put through a fine mesh strainer and cool immediately. Season with a little salt and pepper.
- Preheat the grill: arrange tangerines and Meyer lemons on a plate. Lightly rub with olive oil and sprinkle with black pepper. Grill quickly on one side. Remove and sprinkle fruit with a little balsamic vinegar; set aside for salad. Place greens in a bowl. Season with salt and pepper, sprinkle with Meyer lemon balsamic dressing, and serve.

Serves 4.

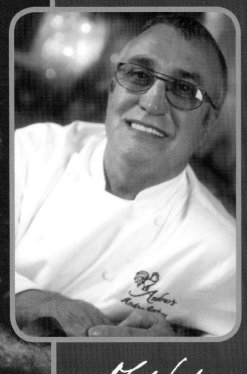

Caramelized Atlantic Salmon with Salmon Caviar, Sour Cream, Lime, and Potato Galette

INGREDIENTS

6 8-ounce pieces of salmon fillet, skinned and deboned

Potato Galette:
2 medium Kennebec potatoes
2 large eggs
1 tablespoon heavy cream
6 ounces butter
1 tablespoon minced chives
3 ounces all-purpose flour
Salt and pepper

Sauce:
¾ cup sour cream
2 tablespoons heavy cream
1 teaspoon salmon caviar
Salt and fresh white pepper
1 lime, juice and zest

Seasoning:
¾ cup sugar
1 teaspoon cayenne pepper
1 ½ teaspoons salt
6 sprigs of dill

DIRECTIONS

Potato Galette:
· Put the potatoes in a pot with enough cold water to cover them and add a little salt.

- Cook the potatoes thoroughly. While the potatoes are still hot, peel and mash them with a food mill. With a whip mix the potatoes, eggs, flour, cream, chives, salt, and pepper. The mix should be soft but not liquid.
- In a heavy-bottomed frying pan, bring the butter to a medium heat. With a serving spoon scoop the mix and place in frying pan to make galette about 3 inches in diameter. You can also use a blinis frying pan, which would form the correct size of galette. Once the galette is brown on 1 side, turn it over and finish cooking slowly. Once cooked, keep the galettes warm until needed.

Sauce:
- In a small saucepan heat up the lime juice. Add the cream and sour cream.
- Season (do not over salt as the salmon caviar will add its share). Add the lime zest. Do not add the caviar until the very last minute.

Salmon:
- Mix all the seasoning ingredients in a bowl. Dip the top side of the salmon in the mixture.
- In a heavy-bottomed frying pan on high heat, put a small amount of vegetable oil, enough to coat the bottom of the pan. Place the salmon on it, the seasoned side down, and let it caramelize. Once caramelized, put the salmon, caramelized side up, on a pregreased small sheet pan and finish cooking in a 380°F oven for 5 minutes.

Presentation:
- Place the warm potato galettes in the center of each hot plate. Place the salmon on the top of the galette, the caramelized side up. Now add the salmon caviar to the sauce; mix in gently. With a spoon, pour some sauce around your salmon. Finish with a sprig of dill on the top of the salmon and serve.

Bon appétit!

Poached Baby Lobster Tails with Crimini Mushroom Custard in a Truffle Tarragon Sauce

Crimini Mushroom Custard:

1 whole egg

2 egg yolks

1 tablespoon butter

2 cloves minced garlic

10 small crimini mushrooms

⅛ cup fresh corn kernels

1 tablespoon mixture chopped thyme and dill

1 ½ cups heavy cream

Salt and freshly ground white pepper

- In medium bowl whisk eggs and yolks until smooth.
- Melt butter in medium pan over low heat. Sauté garlic, mushrooms, and corn until mushrooms are tender but not overcooked.
- Add cream and bring to a simmer. Carefully pour cream and mushroom mixture into blender or food processor. Process mixture until slightly chunky.
- Slowly pour the mushroom cream and herbs into the egg mixture while whisking constantly to temper the egg.
- Pour custard mixture into 6 four-ounce tumble molds. Bake at 400°F in a baking pan with ½ inch of water for approximately 20 minutes or until finished.

Truffle Tarragon Sauce:

2 cloves minced garlic
1 shallot, diced fine
4 ounces white wine
10 ounces lobster stock
12 baby lobster tails
1 tablespoon tarragon
1 tablespoon truffle peelings
5 tablespoons butter
Salt and freshly ground white pepper

- In a saucepan over medium heat, sauté garlic and shallots with 1 tablespoon of butter. Add white wine and reduce by three fourths. Add lobster stock and bring to a simmer. Add lobster tails and poach for approximately 3 minutes or until almost entirely cooked.
- Remove lobster tails from broth. Reserve and keep warm.
- Add tarragon and truffle peelings to broth. Slowly add butter to sauce and season with salt and pepper to taste.

Assembly:

12 steamed red onions, peeled and cut in half lengthwise
30 to 40 baby red potato Parisian balls
2 leeks, white part only, sliced on the bias

- Season all vegetables with butter, salt, and freshly ground white pepper.
- Place custard in center of plate. Cut 2 lobster tails in half and place in center of plate.
- On either side place 2 slices of leek, 1 onion, and 5 potato balls.
- Spoon 2 to 3 ounces of sauce onto plate.

Serves 6.

Club Guastavino's
NYC

Salmon Roasted in Vine Leaves, Grape and Grain Salad, Verjus Vinaigrette

INGREDIENTS

Salmon:

- 8 4-ounce portions salmon filet, all the same thickness, approximately ¾ to 1 inch thick
- 8 to 16 pickled grape leaves, depending on size, available in Middle Eastern markets
- 1 tablespoon ginger, minced
- 1 tablespoon garlic, minced
- 1 tablespoon curry powder
- 1 ½ tablespoons Dijon mustard
- 3 to 7 drops Tabasco
- 4 very thin slices lemon, cut into quarters (pie-slice shaped)
- 1 ½ tablespoons olive oil
- Salt and pepper

Salad:

- 1 cup rye or wheat berries, cooked until tender in 3 to 4 cups water
- 1 cup thinly julienned carrots
- 1 cup assorted seedless grapes: champagne, green, red (large ones cut in half)
- 1 cup Italian parsley, roughly chopped or torn (choose a bunch with smaller, more tender leaves)
- ¾ tablespoon lemon zest, cut with a shredding plane
- 3 to 4 tablespoons roughly chopped tarragon
- ½ to ¾ cup verjus vinaigrette (grape juice from sour grapes available in gourmet shops)

Verjus Vinaigrette:

- ¼ cup verjus
- 2 tablespoons lemon juice
- ¼ cup extra-virgin olive oil
- ¼ teaspoon garlic, minced
- Salt and pepper to taste

112

DIRECTIONS

- Season fish lightly with salt and pepper, remembering that the vine leaves are packed in salted brine.
- Mix the ginger, garlic, curry, mustard, and Tabasco into a paste and smear evenly over the top of the salmon.
- Top each piece of the salmon with a piece of the lemon.
- Lay the vine leaves smooth side down on a counter or cutting board. Place the salmon paste and lemon side down on the leaves and wrap each leaf around the salmon, making sure the fish is completely covered. If the leaves are too small, use 2.
- The salmon can be prepared to this point up to a day in advance and covered and stored in the refrigerator.

To Serve:

- Preheat oven to 550°F.
- Place salmon packages on a baking tray and rub each with a drop or 2 of the olive oil.
- Sprinkle with the verjus and place on the top rack of the oven. Cook 7 to 10 minutes (7 being medium rare and 10 medium well) and remove.
- While the salmon is cooking, toss together the ingredients of the salad and season to taste with salt and freshly cracked pepper.

To Plate:

- Spoon salad in middle of plate and top with salmon.
- Spoon around a little curry, mustard, or basil oil to garnish.
- Package may be torn open at the top for easy access to the salmon and to show the pink interior.

Makes 8 portions, 4 ounces each.

Seafood Cioppino

INGREDIENTS

1 ¼ pounds mussels
32 manila clams
16 jumbo shrimp, cleaned and deveined
12 oysters
2 garlic cloves, minced
2 shallots, minced
3 tablespoons fresh parsley, minced
1 tablespoon fresh rosemary, minced
3 tablespoons fresh basil, minced
1 ½ cups dry red wine
Freshly ground black pepper and salt to taste
12 tomatoes, cored and chopped
Juice of 1 lemon

DIRECTIONS

- Wash the shellfish in salted water and clean the beards from the mussels.
- Shuck the oysters. Set aside in refrigerator.
- In a blender or food processor, purée the tomatoes. Force the purée through the fine screen of a food mill or a fine-meshed sieve. You should have about 3 cups of tomato purée. In a large saucepan, bring the tomato purée to a boil. Set aside and keep warm.
- Add 1 cup of wine to a large pot and bring to a boil. Add the clams and mussels and salt and pepper to taste. Cover and steam just until the shellfish open. Set aside and keep warm.
- Season raw shrimp with salt and pepper. Heat olive oil in sauté pan and sauté the shrimp till evenly cooked on both sides, about 2 minutes per side. Add garlic and shallots and oysters to pan and sauté 1 minute. Add ½ cup of red wine and reduce, approximately 4 minutes. Add this mixture into the pot with the mussels and clams.
- Divide the shellfish equally among 4 large deep plates. Strain the cooking juices from the shellfish into the tomato purée; season with salt and a good amount of pepper. Add the lemon juice and the minced parsley, basil, and rosemary. Spoon the sauce over the hot shellfish and serve.
- Garnish with a parsley sprig and toasted sourdough baguette rubbed with garlic.

Makes 4 servings.

Grilled Lamb and Peach Skewers with Cumin-Raisin Vinaigrette

You might think that combining peaches and lamb in this way is a novel or even original idea. But, in fact, some version of this dish—peaches and lamb grilled together—has probably been served literally millions of times in the Middle East, where lamb and fruit are a classic combination and grilling is an everyday event. So if you have never tried this culinary pairing, you owe it to yourself to make this dish.

As with stew meat, you are going to get better-quality lamb for skewers if you buy a larger cut and cut it into cubes yourself. In this particular instance, we are going to go with two different options for the cut.

Most people will use leg, which is the classic choice for this preparation. But shoulder, while a little chewier, is also a bit more flavorful, so we like that just a bit better. Shoulder arm chops, shoulder blade chops, and shoulder roast are good choices.

Serve with simple rice pilaf, thick slices of grilled bread, and a salad of cucumbers, raisins, and walnuts with a yogurt dressing.

INGREDIENTS

3 tablespoons kosher salt
3 tablespoons freshly cracked black pepper
3 tablespoons cracked coriander seeds (or 1 ½ tablespoons ground coriander)
¼ cup roughly chopped fresh mint
2 tablespoons minced garlic
¼ cup olive oil
2 pounds boneless lamb leg or shoulder, cut into 1-inch cubes
2 red bell peppers, cored, seeded, and cut into eighths
2 red onions, peeled and cut into eighths
2 peaches, pitted and cut into eighths

For the Vinaigrette:
¼ cup golden raisins
½ cup extra-virgin olive oil
¼ cup fresh lime juice (about 2 limes)
3 tablespoons cumin seeds
Kosher salt and freshly cracked black pepper to taste

DIRECTIONS

- Light a fire in your grill.
- In a medium bowl, combine the salt, pepper, coriander, mint, garlic, and olive oil. Dry the lamb cubes with paper towels, add to the bowl, and toss well to coat thoroughly. Thread the meat cubes onto 4 long skewers, alternating them with the peppers, onions, and peaches.
- In a small bowl, combine the vinaigrette ingredients and whisk together well.
- When the fire has died down and the coals are hot (you can hold your hand 5 inches above the grill surface for 1 to 2 seconds), place the skewers on the grill and cook until the vegetables are tender and the lamb is done to your liking, 3 to 4 minutes per side for rare. To check for doneness, nick, peek, and cheat: cut into one of the cubes of meat; it should be slightly less done than you like it. Remove the skewers from the grill and allow to rest for 5 minutes.
- You have two serving options: You can slide the ingredients off the skewers into a large bowl, add the vinaigrette, toss well, and serve. Or you can simply serve each person his or her own skewer, drizzled generously with the vinaigrette.

Serves 4.

Filet of Beef Roasted with Coffee Beans, Pasilla Chile Broth, and Creamy White Grits with Bitter Greens and Wild Mushrooms

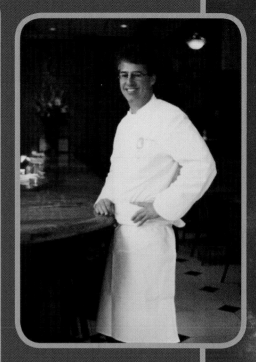

Filet of Beef:

- 2 pounds filet of beef (preferably cut from the large end of the whole filet)
- 1 teaspoon coarse salt
- 1 teaspoon freshly ground pepper
- 2 tablespoons virgin olive oil
- 2 tablespoons very finely ground coffee beans
- 1 tablespoon cocoa powder
- ⅛ teaspoon ground cinnamon

Pasilla Chile Broth:

- 1 tablespoon butter
- ½ large white onion, roughly chopped (8 ounces)
- 4 to 8 garlic cloves, peeled whole
- 2 Pasilla chiles (approximately ½ ounce), stemmed and seeded and torn into large pieces
- 2 ½ cups chicken stock
- 1 thick white corn tortilla (approximately ¾ ounces)
- ¼ cup cream
- 1 teaspoon coarse salt
- 1 teaspoon brown sugar

Creamy White Grits with Bitter Greens and Wild Mushrooms:

4 cups water

1 ¼ cups coarse white grits

1 ½ teaspoons salt

1 tablespoon butter

½ yellow onion, minced

2 garlic cloves, minced

¾ pound shiitake mushrooms, stems removed and caps cut into quarters

4 ounces arugula or other bitter green, roughly chopped

Garnish:

Watercress sprigs

Preparing the Filet:

· Tie the filet of beef with butcher twine at ½-inch intervals. Rub the filet well with the salt and pepper. Rub the filet with the olive oil. Combine the ground coffee, cocoa powder, and cinnamon and mix well. Spread the mixture over a work surface and roll the filet in the mixture to evenly coat the beef. Allow to marinate approximately 30 minutes.

For the Pasilla Chile Broth:

· Heat a saucepan over medium-high heat. Add the butter and sauté the onion and garlic cloves until nicely browned. Add the pieces of Pasilla chile and tortilla pieces and slowly sauté until the ingredients are golden brown. Lower heat to medium low if necessary. Add the chicken stock. Bring the stock to a boil and then simmer, lightly covered, for approximately 10 minutes. Remove from the heat and allow to cool. Transfer the ingredients to a blender and purée for approximately 1 minute or until smooth. Pass the sauce through a sieve to remove any unpuréed pieces. Add the cream, salt, and brown sugar and blend. The sauce should not be thick. If too thick, add some additional chicken stock or water to correct to a very light consistency. Reserve until ready to serve.

Roasting the Filet:

- Preheat an oven to 400°F. Place the filet on a roasting rack in a roasting pan. Roast the filet for 10 minutes at 400°F. Immediately lower the heat to 250°F. After 20 minutes, check the internal temperature of the filet (125°F for medium rare or 135°F for medium). If further cooking is necessary, return the beef to the oven (still set at 250°F) and slowly roast to the desired temperature. Remove the filet from the oven and keep warm. Before carving, remove the string.

Cooking the Grits:

- In a heavy-bottomed 2-quart pot, bring the water to a boil. Add the grits while stirring. Bring the water back to a boil. Lower the heat to a very low simmer. Cover the pot but stir every 2 to 3 minutes until the grits are thick. The grits will take approximately 20 minutes to cook. If the grits become too thick, add a little water to adjust the consistency.

Cooking the Mushrooms and Greens:

- In a skillet over medium-high heat, melt the butter until foaming. Add the chopped onions and garlic. Sauté until the onion is translucent. Add the shiitake mushrooms and sauté until lightly cooked. Add the greens and briefly sauté until wilted. Remove from the heat.

Service:

- When the grits are cooked and ready to serve, stir the greens and mushroom mixture into the grits and keep warm. Slice the filet into ¼-inch-thick slices. Spoon some of the grits into the center of each dinner plate. Arrange the slices of filet around the grits. Ladle some of the Pasilla broth over the filet. Garnish with watercress sprigs.

Serves 4 to 6.

Our Somewhat Famous Jumbo Lump Crab Cakes

INGREDIENTS

1 pound Jumbo Lump Crabmeat
1 tablespoon Meaux Mustard (or good quality whole-grain mustard)
½ egg
½ cup mayonnaise

DIRECTIONS

- Mix the mayonnaise, mustard, and egg.
- Gently fold in the crab.
- Brush a platter lightly with olive oil and carefully form your crab cakes so as not to break the lumps.
- Place into a 500°F oven for 8 to 10 minutes.

The secret of this dish is in the quality of the crabmeat!

Makes 4 cakes.

Royal Daurade (in Olden Way) Cooked in Hen Fat, Lemon, Tomatoes, and Savory

MAIN INGREDIENTS

2 pink daurades, 20 to 25 ounces each
4 tablespoons hen fat

TRIMMING INGREDIENTS

1.7 ounces olive oil
8 ounces chopped onions
2 ounces chopped Paris mushrooms
3 ounces Boletus mushrooms (cépes)
1 cup dry white wine
½ teaspoon thyme
1 tablespoon chopped savory
1 chopped clove of garlic
1.7 ounces lime zest
5 ounces peeled and diced (fresh) tomatoes
Juice of 2 limes
1 stick (4 ounces) butter
Parsley, tarragon, chive
Diced candied lemon (optional)

Chopped Guinea-Fowl:
2.6 ounces guinea-fowl meat
0.6 ounces Bayonne ham
1 teaspoon duck fat
1 teaspoon soy sauce

DECORATING INGREDIENTS

8 laurel leafs
12 lime slices
Chervil peels

DIRECTIONS

- Crisscross the daurade skins with a knife and then paint the surface with the hen fat to fatten the skin.
- Compote the chopped onions in olive oil.
- Brown the mushrooms and then add the diced tomatoes. Mix with the onions. Add the clove of garlic. Moisten with the white wine. Add the thyme and savory. Let this compote stand about 30 minutes.
- Carve the lime zests in very fine juliennes. Blanch 3 times and add to the above compote along with the diced candied lemons (if used).
- Season the daurades with salt and pepper and cover with the lime slices and the laurel leaves.
- Put the compote in a deep ovenproof dish, add the daurades, and place in a hot oven for 15 minutes.
- Finely chop the guinea-fowl meat and the Bayonne ham. Brown quickly in the goose fat. When cooked, bind with soy sauce.
- Strain the compote and divide among the serving plates; place the daurades on the plates and keep warm.
- To the strained compote, add the lime juice and the chopped herbs. Cover the daurades and sprinkle with the chervil peels and the chopped guinea-fowl.

Serves 4.

Salmon and Shiitake Hash

INGREDIENTS

6 tablespoons vegetable oil
1 medium onion, peeled and finely chopped
2 cups shiitake mushrooms, stems removed and quartered
1 teaspoon garlic, one clove peeled and finely chopped
3 cups potatoes, cooked and peeled
1 ¼ pounds salmon, cooked or smoked, skinned, boned, and flaked
½ cup sour cream
1 lemon, zest and juice
2 tablespoons fresh dill, chopped
Sea salt and freshly ground pepper to taste

METHOD

- Place half of the oil in a heavy skillet over high heat. When hot, add the onion and sauté until slightly crunchy, 3 to 5 minutes. Add the mushrooms and cook until just wilted, about 2 minutes. Add the garlic and sauté for 1 minute. Remove to a mixing bowl and set aside.
- In the same skillet, add the remaining oil, bring to medium heat, and add the potatoes. Cook until the edges are just crisp, about 5 minutes. Remove from the heat and mix with the reserved onions and add the rest of the ingredients. Season to taste with the salt and pepper and mix well but do not pack the mixture.
- Return the mixture to a skillet and cook over medium heat, tossing to prevent the hash from sticking. Remove to a warm plate and serve.
- Garnish the hash with anything you like best, from sour cream to poached eggs to salmon caviar to chopped scallions. Serve over bitter greens such as sautéed Swiss chard.

Serves 4 to 6.

MEAT, POULTRY, & FISH

Coscia Di Pollo Ripiena
Stuffed Chicken Leg

INGREDIENTS

11 ounces of chicken leg (deboned)
¼ teaspoon salt
½ teaspoon black pepper
2 tablespoons olive oil
1 medium onion, sliced (5 ounces)
4 garlic cloves
4 sage leaves
1 cup Madeira wine
½ cup veal glaze
Stuffing:
4 artichoke hearts, thinly sliced (5 ounces)
¼ cup olive oil
½ teaspoon salt
½ teaspoon pepper
2 garlic cloves
1 ounce proscuitto, julienned

PREPARE

- Preheat oven to 400°F.
- To prepare stuffing, heat olive oil in a medium saucepan. When the oil is hot, add artichokes, garlic, salt, and pepper. Sauté until garlic turns golden brown in color (5 minutes). Remove from heat and drain oil. Pass the contents through a strainer and allow them to cool. Take the cooled mixture and combine it with the proscuitto in a mixing bowl. Blend well.
- Take chicken leg and sprinkle the inside with ½ teaspoon of black pepper and ¼ teaspoon of salt. Stuff leg with the mixture. Tie the leg with cooking twine. In a medium saucepan, heat the olive oil over medium heat. When the oil is hot, add the chicken leg. Sprinkle with ¼ teaspoon each of salt and pepper. Sauté the leg for 1 minute on each side and add the onions, garlic, and sage. Cook for 1 minute. Add Madeira and cook until the alcohol burns off. When the alcohol has been reduced, remove the pan from the heat and add veal glaze. Place the pan in the preheated oven and bake for 20 minutes.
- After 20 minutes, remove the pan from the heat. Place the chicken aside. Place the pan back over medium heat and bring its contents to a boil. Remove from the heat and transfer to a blender. Purée until smooth.

124

Serve:
- Remove cooking twine and slice stuffed leg. Serve over a bed of sauce.

Tuna Milanese with Wilted Spinach, Proscuitto, Mushrooms, and Pine Nuts

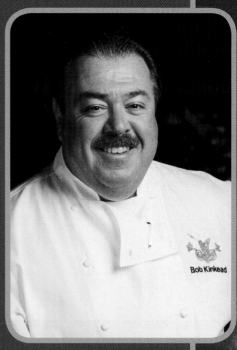

INGREDIENTS

6 each tuna paillards, 5- to 6-ounce portions
½ inch thick
⅔ cup raisins
1 cup port
3 cups bread crumbs
¼ cup Parmesan, grated
½ cup olive oil
½ cup clarified butter
¼ cup extra-virgin olive oil
⅛ cup unsalted butter
12 medium mushrooms, quartered
1 pound spinach, picked and washed (loosely packed)
½ cup pine nuts, toasted
2 cloves garlic, minced
¼ pound proscuitto, sliced thin and cut into julienne
½ cup red wine vinegar
1 ounce lemon juice
½ cup Parmesan, shredded
1 medium red onion, julienned
Salt and pepper
½ cup Caper Parsley Relish (recipe follows)

DIRECTIONS

· Cut thin tuna steaks (or have fishmonger do it). Do not buy thick cuts and pound to ½-inch thickness like you would veal. Tuna is too delicate.

· In a saucepan, poach the raisins in the port until plump. Drain and reserve the raisins.

· Mix the bread crumbs, shredded Parmesan, olive oil, and if desired, some chopped parsley together with salt and pepper and set aside to bread tuna.

- Mix the extra-virgin olive oil and the clarified butter. Salt and pepper the tuna paillards and dredge in the oil-butter mixture. Dip again into the bread crumbs, thoroughly coating both sides.
- In a sauté pan over medium to high heat, add a little oil and when hot add the butter. Add the breaded paillards and sauté on one side about 3 minutes until brown and crisp. Turn and cook the other side until brown and crisp. Keep warm. Make sure not to crowd the sauté pan. You will probably be able to cook only 2 paillards at a time.
- When paillards are cooked, wipe out the pan, add a little oil (or left over butter/oil mixture) to the pan. Add in the garlic and cook 2 minutes. Add the mushroom quarters and sauté until browned. Add in the spinach, pine nuts, proscuitto, and let start to wilt. Remove from the heat.
- In a stainless bowl add the raisins, onions, shredded Parmesan, and wilted spinach mixture, dress with the vinegar, and toss.
- On 6 warm dinner plates, divide the spinach mixture and sprinkle on the lemon juice. Top each with a tuna paillard and top each paillard with the parsley caper relish. Serve warm with a lemon crown.

Parsley Caper Relish

INGREDIENTS

2 bunches Italian parsley, leaves picked, coarsely chopped
2 lemons, peeled and sectioned, seeded and diced
¼ cup capers
¼ cup extra-virgin olive oil
1 tablespoon red wine vinegar
Salt and pepper
- Mix all together.

Serves 6.

Meatballs with Parsnip Gratin

INGREDIENTS

½ cup fine dry bread crumbs
¾ cup heavy cream
1 ½ tablespoons olive oil
1 medium yellow onion, minced
⅔ cup ground beef
⅔ cup ground veal
⅔ cup ground pork
2 tablespoons honey
1 large egg
Kosher salt and freshly ground black pepper

DIRECTIONS

- In a small bowl, combine bread crumbs and ½ cup heavy cream. Stir with fork until smooth. Set aside.
- Heat the oil in a small pan over medium heat and add the onion. Sauté until softened but not browned, about 5 minutes.
- In a large bowl, combine beef, veal, pork, honey, cooked onions, and egg. Season with salt and pepper to taste. Add the bread crumb and cream mixture to the meat and mix well.
- With wet hands (to keep the meat from sticking), shape a meatball the size of a golf ball. If the meat is too soft to shape, more bread crumbs may be added to the mixture. Continue shaping meatballs, placing on a plate brushed with water.
- In a large skillet over medium-high heat, melt the butter and add the meatballs. Sauté, browning on all sides, until cooked through, about 7 minutes. Remove to a plate and discard the fat from the skillet.

Parsnip Gratin:

5 parsnips, peeled and thinly sliced

4 Idaho potatoes, peeled

1 Spanish onion

½ quart cream

4 sprigs thyme

1 tablespoon butter

½ cup Parmesan cheese

1 ½ quarts milk

- In a pot, place the potatoes, milk, onion, and garlic; boil until soft and purée.
- Slice the parsnips into thin slices using a mandolin.
- Butter a deep dish.
- Layer the potato purée, thyme, and parsnips.
- Pour the cream over and sprinkle the Parmesan cheese.
- Bake for 45 minutes at 350°F.

Makes approximately 24 servings.

Napa Style Sole Veronique

INGREDIENTS

3 tablespoons extra-virgin olive oil
1 pound sole filet, skinned and boned
½ cup Wondra flour (or all-purpose flour)
2 tablespoons shallots, minced
1 teaspoon fresh thyme leaves
½ cup chardonnay grape juice
⅔ cup seedless red grapes
2 tablespoons sweet butter
Gray salt and black pepper to taste

DIRECTIONS

- In a skillet large enough to hold the fish filet(s), heat 2 tablespoons of the olive oil on medium-high heat until just smoking.
- While the oil is heating, season the sole with salt and pepper and lightly dredge on both sides in the flour. Carefully place the fish in the hot oil. Cook until golden brown, about 4 minutes and then carefully turn the fish over and continue to cook for another 30 seconds. Transfer the fish to a warm plate and hold.
- Add the remaining olive oil to the pan, adjust the heat to medium, and add the shallots. Sauté for about 2 minutes until lightly caramelized and then add the thyme. Add the grape juice and stir with the pan ingredients to incorporate.
- Use a wooden spoon to scrape the bottom of the pan to free any ingredient that adheres. Adjust the heat so that the juice is reduced by half in a soft boil. Add the grapes and warm in the sauce. Melt the butter into the sauce and adjust the seasoning to taste. Spoon the grapes over the warm fish filets and then finish with the sauce. Serve immediately.

Makes 2 to 3 servings.

Chardonnay grape juice and gray salt can be purchased on Chef Michael Chiarello's Web site at: www.napastyle.com.

MEAT, POULTRY, & FISH

– CHEF ALESSANDRO STRATTA –

Braised Short Ribs of Beef with Creamy Horseradish Potatoes

For the Short Ribs:

4 16-ounce short ribs of beef
½ cup onion, diced
½ cup garlic, diced
½ cup carrot, diced
2 tablespoons thyme
¼ cup lavender honey
½ cup sherry vinegar
1 bottle rich red wine
1 quart chicken stock
2 tablespoons butter
2 tablespoons olive oil
Salt and pepper to taste

Preparing the Short Ribs:

- Preheat oven to 300°F. Heat a heavy saucepan over high heat. Season ribs well with salt and pepper. Add olive oil and get to smoking hot and sear the short ribs well on both sides. Once browned, add the diced vegetables. Cook until light golden brown. Add honey and caramelize and deglaze with the vinegar and reduce until liquid evaporates. Add the red wine and reduce to one third. Add the chicken stock and bring to a boil. Bake in oven until meat is very tender (should pull off the bone). Reduce cooking liquid until it is thick and coats the back of a spoon. Strain sauce on to cooked ribs. Cover and keep warm. Finish with butter just before serving.

For the Creamy Potatoes:

8 large Idaho potatoes
2 quarts heavy cream
4 tablespoons prepared horseradish purée
Salt and pepper to taste

130

Preparing the Creamy Potatoes:
- Peel the potatoes and slice them one eighth-inch thick (crosswise). Mix the horseradish with the cream and seasonings. Toss the sliced potatoes into cream and coat well. Layer potatoes into a 2-inch-deep pan and cover to ¼ to ½-inch with cream. Bake at 350°F for 2 hours or until potatoes are thoroughly cooked and the tops are golden brown. Once cooked, wrap with tin foil and keep in a warm place until needed.

For the Candied Shallots:
8 large shallots, peeled
1 tablespoon honey
2 tablespoons sherry vinegar
1 cup port wine
1 tablespoon olive oil
Salt and pepper to taste

Preparing the Candied Shallots:
- Heat a sauté pan over medium heat and add the oil. Allow oil to smoke and add the peeled shallots. Sauté and lightly color evenly. Season and add honey. Caramelize and deglaze with vinegar. Reduce until liquid evaporates and then add the port wine. Simmer and reduce to a syrup with shallots until thoroughly coated. Add the glazed shallots to the short ribs and sauce.

Presenting the Dish:
- Scoop out a large spoonful of creamy potatoes and place on a plate. Place the short ribs and shallots around and spoon sauce over meat. Serve hot.

Serves 4.

Coriander Breast of Duck with Sweet Potato Sauce

Base Sauce:

9 cups sweet potato juice
4 tablespoons fresh ginger
2 chopped Thai chili peppers
Salt, pepper, and freshly squeezed lemon juice to taste

- Allow the juice to stand 4 hours. This will allow much of the potato starch in the juice to settle. Pour the juice through a fine mesh strainer, being careful to leave the settled starch behind. Place over a medium flame and reduce to approximately 1 ½ to 2 cups or until the sauce naturally thickens. Remove from the fire and stir in the ginger and Thai chili pepper. Stir until the sauce tastes spicy enough and strain immediately. Season to taste with salt, pepper, and lemon juice.

Yield: approximately 1½ cups.

Coriander Breast of Duck:

2 tablespoons toasted coriander seeds, crushed
4 skinless, boneless duck breasts, approximately 5 to 7 ounces each
1 ½ cups sweet potato sauce base
2 medium skin-on parsnips poached for 15 minutes
1 medium sweet potato, cut into one eighth wedges
1 tablespoon grapeseed oil
Salt and pepper to taste
4 sprigs baby pea shoots

- Split each poached parsnip in half, lengthwise and rub with a small amount of grapeseed oil. Rub the 8 sweet potato wedges with grapeseed oil. Season the parsnip and potato with salt and pepper. Bake on a sheet tray in a preheated 400°F oven until browned and cooked through (approximately 15 minutes). Split each parsnip in half lengthwise.
- Heat a large, nonstick sauté pan over a medium heat. Season each duck breast with salt and pepper. Press one side of the duck breast into the coriander seeds. Use a squeeze bottle to drizzle a thin line of grapeseed oil over the coriander on each duck breast. Add the duck breasts, seed side down, to the hot sauté pan. Sauté until the coriander browns. Turn the duck breasts over and set the pan off the flame for 3 to 5 minutes. Remove the breasts and allow them to rest 2 to 4 minutes.
- To plate, set a piece of parsnip and wedge of sweet potato on each plate. Slice each duck breast into quarter-inch slices and arrange against the vegetables. Spoon sauce onto each plate and garnish with pea shoots.

Yields 4 servings.

Pan-Seared Halibut with Ragout of Chanterelles, Fresh Peas, Oven-Dried Tomatoes, Pearl Onions, Baby Fennel, and Crunchy Potatoes

INGREDIENTS

4 to 6 ounces halibut steaks, cleaned
4 Roma tomatoes, peeled, halved, and seeded
½ cup fresh peas, shelled and blanched
12 pearl onions, peeled
½ cup Chanterelle mushrooms, cleaned
4 baby fennel
1 cup russet potatoes, peeled and cubed
½ cup fish fumet, reduced
4 ounces butter, cubed
1 teaspoon sugar
1 cup water
Shallots, chopped
Garlic, chopped
White wine
Olive oil
Thyme, fresh
Salt and pepper

DIRECTIONS

To Oven-Dry the Tomatoes:
- Line a cookie pan with aluminum foil and spray with olive oil.
- Place halved tomatoes on pan and sprinkle both sides with salt, pepper, and fresh thyme leaves.

- Drizzle olive oil over tomatoes and arrange skin side up on the pan.
- Place pan in 200°F oven for 1 to 2 hours to remove water and concentrate flavor.
- Set aside.

For the Vegetables:

- Pearl onions: heat olive oil in pan; add onions and 1 teaspoon sugar. Swirl onions in pan and add 1 cup water. When onions are soft, set aside in the cooking liquid.
- Baby fennel: heat olive oil in pan; add fennel, white wine, and thyme sprigs. Simmer until fennel is cooked through. Set aside in the cooking liquid.
- Chanterelles: heat olive oil in sauté pan; add chopped shallots and garlic. Add chanterelles and sauté until the water is released and mushrooms are cooked.
- Potatoes: heat olive oil and fry potatoes at the last moment.

For the Halibut:

- Heat olive oil in sauté pan and sear halibut on both sides. Transfer pan to 425°F oven and finish cooking.

To Serve:

- Mix all of the vegetables together, including the tomatoes and potatoes.
- Bring half of the vegetable cooking liquid and the fish fumet to a boil. Whisk in the butter.
- Place the vegetable ragout in the center of the plate and the halibut on top. Ladle the sauce over the fish and serve immediately.

Serves 4.

Roast Beef Tenderloin Stuffed with Swiss Chard, Oyster Mushrooms, Sun-Dried Tomatoes, and Mozzarella Cheese Served with Garlic-Whipped New Potatoes and Balsamic Vinegar Marsala Jus©

INGREDIENTS

Beef:

1 36- to 40-ounce center cut beef tenderloin, all fat trimmed

1 tablespoon of The Body Gourmet Sweet Porcini Pleasure Healthy Spice Blend

¼ pound Swiss chard, leaves only, washed and roughly cut

¼ pound button mushrooms, stemmed and thinly sliced

½ cup sun-dried tomatoes, rehydrated in hot water and thinly sliced

1 ½ tablespoons pine nuts

¼ pound low-fat part-skim mozzarella cheese

Cracked black pepper to taste

Potatoes:

1 ¼ pounds red new potatoes, washed and cut into quarters

10 cloves garlic, peeled

Cracked pepper to taste

Balsamic Vinegar Marsala Jus:

1 cup balsamic vineger

1 cup marsala wine

1 cup chicken broth, low sodium

METHOD

- Beef: heat a large nonstick Teflon pan. Add mushrooms and sauté until half cooked. Add sun-dried tomatoes and pine nuts and cook for 1 minute. Add Swiss chard and cook until wilted. Add cheese and cracked pepper. Pull off heat and allow to cool to room temperature. Using a long slicing knife, take beef and cut an incision through the middle the long way. Do this on both ends. Insert your fingers through the loin from both ends. Move fingers around and create a pocket that connects from both ends. You should form a tubelike area approximately 1 inch in diameter that runs from end to end of the tenderloin. Now push stuffing into this cavity from both ends and form an even amount throughout. Do it a little at a time and use the back end of a rubber spatula to push the mixture through the loin. When cavity is filled, season loin with cracked pepper.
- Season the outside of the tenderloin with the Body Gourmet Sweet Porcini Pleasure Healthy Spice Blend. Sear the beef tenderloin on all sides until golden brown. Roast in the oven on a sheet pan at 350°F for 20 to 30 minutes or until desired temperature is reached. While beef is roasting, make syrup and potatoes. When beef is cooked, allow to rest for 5 to 7 minutes before slicing.
- Syrup: in a saucepan, add balsamic vinegar and marsala. Bring liquid to a boil and turn down to a simmer. Reduce the volume by two thirds. Add chicken broth and again reduce the volume by two thirds. You should have a nice sauce consistency.
- Potatoes: add potatoes and garlic to a saucepan and fill with water. Boil until tender. Drain and discard water. Whip potatoes with 2 forks until fluffy but still chunky. Season with cracked black pepper.
- To plate: slice beef into 12 slices. Place potatoes on the top of the plate and fan beef in front. Pour sauce around the beef and enjoy.

The Body Gourmet spice blends can be purchased on Chef Jim Shiebler's Web site at www.thebodygourmet.com.

All the best,
Gloria Loring

Chicken with 40 Cloves of Garlic

Put in a Large Baking Pan with Lid:
2 ½ cups chopped onions
1 teaspoon dried thyme
6 chopped parsley sprigs
4 celery stalks cut in 2-inch pieces

Add:
8 chicken thighs and 8 legs, skinned
½ cup white wine or vermouth
Salt and pepper
Dash of nutmeg
Juice of 1 large lemon

Tuck in around the Chicken:
40 cloves of garlic, unpeeled
· Cover with foil and then top with the lid.
· Bake at 375°F for 1 ½ hours.

138

Grilled Whole Branzino with Shaved Fennel and Orange Salad

PREPARATION

Branzino is a Mediterranean fish with tender flaky flesh and sweet, juicy flavor. The fish can be bought whole, gutted, and scaled. Simply brush the exterior of the whole fish with olive oil and season with salt and freshly ground pepper. Place the fish on the open wood-fired grill over medium heat and let it cook evenly on one side for about 4-5 minutes without touching it and then roll the whole fish over with a large spatula and cook on the second side for another 4 minutes or so or until the skin is crispy on both sides and the fish seems like it would come apart with a nudge of the fork. Serve on top of fennel and orange salad and dress the fish with the green olive vinaigrette. A Blue Room favorite.

Salad (served under the grilled fish):

Shaved fennel (per serving to your liking), half bulb
Orange sections (per serving to your liking), 1 orange
Watercress (per serving to your liking), half bunch
1 tablespoon orange juice
2 tablespoon extra-virgin olive oil
Salt and pepper to taste
· Toss the watercress, orange sections, and fennel in orange juice vinaigrette and place on plate after fish has been prepared.

Green Olive Vinaigrette:

1 cup extra-virgin olive oil
½ cup lemon
1 cup green olives (pitted and chopped)
1 teaspoon toasted coriander
1 teaspoon chop tarragon
Salt and pepper to taste

DESSERTS

Nancy Bell

This is a "health-food" recipe.

It's fabulously high in fiber and betacarotene. I also find it delicious and satisfying.

– NANCY BELL –

Aunt Erin's Squash Pie

Crust:
- ¾ cup oat flakes or oatmeal
- ¾ cup whole wheat pastry flour
- ¼ cup brown rice flour
- ¼ cup walnuts, sunflower seeds, or shelled pumpkin seeds, chopped
- 2 tablespoons sesame oil
- ¼ teaspoon salt
- ⅓ to ½ cup water
- Mix all ingredients with a fork. Press with fingers into an 8- or 9-inch pie pan. Bake 10 minutes at 350°F. Remove and set aside.

Filling:
- 1 large butternut squash (can also use red khuri, pumpkin, or a couple of acorn squashes)
- 1 tablespoon honey
- 2 tablespoons lemon juice
- 1 ½ teaspoons cinnamon
- ¼ teaspoon allspice
- Pinch of ground cloves
- ¼ teaspoon salt
- Cut squash into quarters and steam until tender.
- With a fork, mash hot squash meat together with other ingredients. Spoon onto baked crust. Sprinkle top with a few sesame seeds and bake at 400°F for 1 hour.

Chocolate Ladyfinger Ice Box Cake

INGREDIENTS

4 squares unsweetened chocolate
¼ cup water
1 cup granulated sugar
6 eggs, separated
½ pound sweet butter
1 ½ cups powdered sugar
2 tablespoons vanilla
About 2 ½ dozen ladyfingers

DIRECTIONS

- Melt chocolate and then add water and granulated sugar. When thick, add well-beaten egg yolks. Cool.
- Cream butter with powdered sugar. Add chocolate mixture to this with vanilla. Fold in stiffly beaten egg whites.
- Line bottom and sides of greased 9- or 10-inch springform pan with ladyfingers and pour mixture into pan. Arrange remaining ladyfingers attractively on top. Refrigerate overnight.
- Serve topped with sweetened whipped cream and chocolate decorettes.

It is very rich, very, very special, and very, very, very good! It came from my mother-in-law and has been a family favorite for years.

– BEVERLY GARLAND –

Chocolate Meringue Torte

Cinnamon Meringue Shell:

3 egg whites at room temperature
¼ teaspoon salt
¼ teaspoon cream of tartar
¾ cup sugar
½ teaspoon cinnamon

- Preheat oven to 275°F.
- Cover a cookie sheet with a piece of foil; draw an 8-inch circle in center.
- Beat egg whites, salt, and cream of tartar until soft peaks form. Blend sugar and cinnamon and gradually add to egg whites, beating until very stiff peaks form and all sugar is dissolved.
- Spread within the circle, making the bottom ½ inch thick and mounding around edge, making it ¾ inch high.
- Bake in slow oven for 1 hour. Turn off heat and let dry in oven with oven door closed about 2 hours. Peel off paper carefully.

Filling:

1 6-ounce package (1 cup) semi-sweet chocolate pieces
2 beaten egg yolks
¼ cup water
1 cup whipping cream
¼ cup sugar
¼ teaspoon cinnamon

- Melt the chocolate over hot, not boiling, water. Cool slightly and then spread 2 tablespoons of the chocolate over bottom of cooled meringue shell.
- To remaining chocolate, add egg yolks and water and blend. Chill until mixture is thick.
- Combine cream, sugar, and cinnamon; whip until stiff. Spread half over chocolate in shell; fold remainder into chocolate mixture and spread on top.
- Trim with whipped cream and a few pecans if desired.

Serves 8.

B.B.'s German Chocolate Double Delight

INGREDIENTS

4 ounces German
  sweet chocolate
1 cup butter
4 egg yolks, unbeaten
2 ½ cups cake flour
1 teaspoon baking soda
4 egg whites, stiffly
  beaten

½ cup boiling water
2 cups sugar
1 teaspoon vanilla
½ teaspoon salt
1 cup buttermilk

DIRECTIONS

- Melt the chocolate over boiling water and let cool.
- Cream the butter and sugar until fluffy.
- Add egg yolks, one at a time, and beat well after each addition.
- Add the melted chocolate and vanilla; mix well.
- Sift flour, salt, and baking soda and add alternately with buttermilk to chocolate mixture, beating until smooth after each addition.
- Fold in the beaten egg whites.
- Pour into three 8- or 9-inch layer pans lined with parchment paper and bake at 350°F for 30 to 40 minutes.
- Cool and frost middle and top only with coconut-pecan frosting.

B.B.'s Coconut-Pecan Frosting

1 cup evaporated milk
1 cup sugar
3 egg yolks
½ cup butter or margarine
1 teaspoon vanilla
1 ⅓ cups coconut, shredded
1 cup chopped pecans

- In a saucepan, combine milk, sugar, egg yolks, butter, and vanilla.
- Cook over medium heat, stirring constantly until thickened.
- Add coconut and pecans and beat until thick enough to spread.

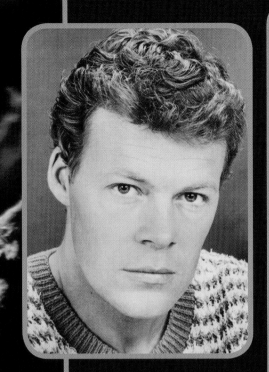

Being an actor, I'm on the go a lot. Most of my days are spent on location, usually on a movie set. That usually means quite a bit of catered food. Sometimes I come home, and I'm too tired to cook. Being single, it can be a bother to rustle up food for one. So my eating habits are sporadic. However, one of my favorite ways to relax—a sort of respite from the hectic Hollywood life—is to have a friend or two over for a fancy dessert and a chilled bottle of wine, maybe running an old classic film on the VCR. If I had a special romantic night, I might serve up the following.

Julian's Treat Mousse Tart Topped with Strawberries

Cocoa Crust Ingredients:

¾ cup all-purpose flour
⅓ cup confectioner's sugar
¼ cup unsweetened cocoa powder
⅓ cup butter-flavored solid vegetable shortening
2 tablespoons cold water

Mousse Filling:

1 pint fresh strawberries, rinsed, hulled, and cut lengthwise
1 tablespoon instant coffee granules or powder
1 box chocolate-flavored mousse mix
1 cup milk

To Prepare Crust:

- Use a 9-inch tart pan with removable bottom. Heat oven to 425°F.
- Mix flour, sugar, and cocoa in medium-sized bowl. Cut in shortening with pastry blender or 2 knives until mixture resembles coarse crumbs. Stir in water until well distributed.
- Gather dough in ball, flatten, and then press evenly over bottom and then up sides of ungreased tart pan until pastry extends ⅛ of an inch above the sides. Prick holes in bottom.
- Bake about 10 minutes until firm to touch or until pastry is set. Allow to cool on rack.

To Prepare Filling:

- Pour the milk into a deep 1 ½-quart bowl; add the mousse mix and the instant coffee. Use electric mixer or beat by hand until blended. Beat about 3 minutes on high speed until the mixture thickens. Spread in the cooled crust. Refrigerate a couple of hours until the mousse has set.
- Lay out strawberry halves on top shortly before serving time.

Serves 8.

– GENERAL H. NORMAN SCHWARZKOPF –

Brenda Schwarzkopf's Sour Cream Peach Pie

Preparation time: 10 to 25 minutes
Cooking time: 30 to 40 minutes

INGREDIENTS

2 pounds fresh peaches (or 1 large can sliced
   peaches, drained)
2 tablespoons cornstarch (use only with fresh peaches)
¼ cup apple juice (use only with fresh peaches)
⅓ cup flour
½ cup sugar (if using fresh peaches, you might
   want to increase to ¾ cup)
¼ teaspoon salt
1 cup sour cream
1 9-inch deep-dish pie shell, unbaked
1 tablespoon sugar and ¼ teaspoon cinnamon, mixed
Peach slices for garnish

DIRECTIONS

- Preheat oven to 350°F.
- Peel and slice peaches (10 to 12 slices each);
  place in large bowl. If using fresh peaches, mix
  cornstarch and apple juice until smooth. Pour
  over peaches; toss gently to coat. Let stand
  10 to 15 minutes. (Or drain canned peaches
  thoroughly; place in bowl.)
- Mix flour, sugar, salt, and sour cream.
- Arrange peaches in pie shell; top with sour cream
  mixture. Sprinkle with sugar and cinnamon.
- Bake 30 to 40 minutes, until crust is lightly
  browned. Garnish with peach slices if desired.

Makes 10 servings.

Stuffed Date Drops

INGREDIENTS

1 pound (about 70) pitted dates
1 3-ounce package pecan or walnut halves
¼ cup shortening
¾ cup medium brown sugar
1 egg
1 ¼ cups sifted enriched flour
½ teaspoon baking powder
½ teaspoon baking soda
¼ teaspoon salt
¼ cup sour cream

DIRECTIONS

- Stuff dates with nut halves.
- Cream shortening and sugar until light. Beat in egg.
- Sift sugar, flour, baking powder, soda, and salt. Add alternately with sour cream to creamed mixture. Stir in dates.
- Drop onto greased cookie sheet (1 date per cookie). Bake at 400°F for 8 to 10 minutes. Place on a rack to cool.
- Top with Golden Glow frosting.

Yields 5 ¼ dozen cookies.

Golden Glow Frosting:
½ cup butter or margarine
3 cups powdered sugar
¾ teaspoon vanilla
About 3 tablespoons water

- Lightly brown butter or margarine and remove from heat.
- Gradually beat in the powdered sugar and vanilla. Slowly add water until mixture is spreading consistency.

This recipe yields enough to frost your delicious cookies.

Julie's Scone Recipe

INGREDIENTS

2 ⅓ cups unbleached all-purpose flour
1 ½ teaspoons cream of tartar
¾ teaspoon baking soda
1 teaspoon salt
1 stick of butter (½ cup)
⅓ cup sugar
½ cup raisins
½ cup sour cream
½ cup buttermilk
1 egg and 1 egg yolk

DIRECTIONS

- Preheat oven to 425°F. Grease baking sheet.
- Sift together flour, tartar, soda, sugar, and salt twice. Rub in butter to look like "coarse" meal.
- Beat egg and yolk and add to buttermilk and sour cream.
- Put "well hole" in dry mixture and add liquid mixture plus raisins. Don't overmix.
- Flour a large sheet of wax paper and also put flour on your hands. Pat dough flat to ¼ to ½-inch thick. Cut circles in dough about 2 inches in diameter and then lay out on baking sheet in 2 layers like 2 cookies stacked on top of each other. (This stacking makes the scones easier to cut.)
- Bake at 425°F for 12 to 15 minutes.

Makes about 10 to 12 scones.

— MARJ DUSAY —

Sour Milk Chocolate Cake

INGREDIENTS

½ cup butter
2 cups sugar
2 eggs
1 cup sour milk (use buttermilk)
2 ½ cups flour

1 teaspoon baking soda (heaping)
⅔ cup cocoa in ½ cup boiling water
1 teaspoon vanilla

DIRECTIONS

- Cream together butter, sugar, and eggs until well combined. Add sour milk.
- Stir together baking soda and cocoa in boiling water and add to other ingredients. Then add flour and vanilla.
- Bake at 350°F. Layer cake pans, bake 30 to 35 minutes; oblong pan, bake 35 to 45 minutes or more. Try a toothpick test in the middle of the cake. If it comes out clean, cake is done. Choose icing.

Icing:

½ cup melted butter
2 ounces melted chocolate (melt in a little coffee)
1 ⅓ cups powdered sugar
1 teaspoon vanilla
1 scant teaspoon lemon juice
1 cup nuts
Enough cream to get the right consistency

- Mix all ingredients together and frost cake as desired.

Brown Sugar Icing:

6 tablespoons brown sugar
4 tablespoons white sugar
4 tablespoons butter
5 tablespoons cream

- Bring ingredients to a boil and boil for 1 minute. Set aside to cool and then beat. Frost cake.

Fudge Frosting:

2 cups sugar
2 squares chocolate
⅔ cup milk

1 tablespoon butter
1 teaspoon vanilla
Dash of salt

- Combine all ingredients except vanilla. Cook to softball stage and add vanilla.
- Beat until creamy and thick; spread on cool cake.

150

Cranberry Pudding also Known as Steamed Cranberry Cake

Jerry Ver Dorn
"Ross Marler"

INGREDIENTS

½ cup mild molasses
2 teaspoons baking soda
¼ cup hot water
Dash of salt
1 ½ cups flour
2 cups raw cranberries

To Prepare Cake:

- Pour molasses into a large mixing bowl.
- Dissolve baking soda in ¼ cup hot water and stir into molasses (it will foam up). Stir in salt, flour, and cranberries.
- Put batter into a greased loaf pan and cover tightly with 2 layers of foil. Secure foil around rim of loaf pan with a heavy rubber band or string.
- Place loaf pan on a steamer rack or inverted plate in a Dutch oven casserole with water up to the bottom of the loaf pan. Cover and steam for 1 hour and 40 minutes, adding more water to Dutch oven if necessary. Batter turns into a rich, dark cake.
- Cool and remove from loaf pan if desired.

Topping:

½ cup butter or margarine
1 cup sugar
1 cup whipping cream
1 teaspoon vanilla

- Combine ingredients in saucepan and boil slowly for 20 minutes, stirring occasionally. Remove from heat and stir in vanilla.
- Serve hot over warm cranberry pudding slices.

Both pudding and topping can be made ahead, cooled, and refrigerated. Reheat (in microwave) when ready to serve.

– ROSIE O'DONNELL –

Rosie's Marshmallow Mud Squares

INGREDIENTS

Cake:

2 cups sugar

1 cup shortening

4 eggs

3 teaspoons vanilla

1 ½ cups flour

⅓ cup cocoa

⅓ teaspoon salt

1 6 ½-ounce bag mini-marshmallows

Frosting:

2 sticks butter, room temperature

½ cup cocoa

1 box powdered sugar

1 teaspoon vanilla

½ cup evaporated milk

DIRECTIONS

- Preheat the oven to 300°F. Grease and flour a 9-by 13-inch glass baking dish.
- In the bowl of an electric mixer, add sugar and shortening and cream together. Add eggs and vanilla and beat 30 seconds.
- In a separate bowl, sift the flour, cocoa, and salt together. Add to the mixture and beat until well combined. Pour the mixture into the glass baking dish, place in the oven, and bake for 35 minutes.
- Make the frosting while the cake is baking. In the bowl of an electric mixer, beat the butter, cocoa, powdered sugar, and vanilla together. Slowly add the milk. Set aside.
- Once cake is baked, remove pan from the oven. Spread the marshmallows on top of the cake and return the pan to the oven for 5 more minutes. Remove the pan from the oven and cool for a few minutes.
- Evenly apply the frosting. Allow this to stand about 2 hours before cutting into squares.

Note: If the marshmallows are too hot, the frosting will sink right through. The frosting should be the top layer. It will look a little darker once it hits the heat of the cake.

– MARILYN TUCKER QUAYLE –

Fried Biscuits

INGREDIENTS

2 cups milk, scalded
1 package yeast in ½ cup warm water
4 rounded tablespoons sugar
3 tablespoons margarine or lard
1 tablespoon salt
6 cups flour

DIRECTIONS

- After yeast has dissolved and set for 5 minutes, mix all ingredients together in the order they appear in the recipe, reserving ½ cup flour to use while kneading.
- Knead the dough for 5 minutes. Let rise covered in a greased crock or bowl in a warm place until doubled in bulk. Punch down, knead again, and let rise a second time in greased crock or bowl until doubled in bulk. Punch down and gently knead for 1 minute.
- Spread dough out on a floured board until ¾ of an inch thick. Cut with donut hole cutter or with a 6-ounce orange juice can into biscuits. Have ready a deep fat fryer or large saucepan with at least 3 inches of hot Crisco shortening. Gently ease biscuits into hot oil, turning as they cook to ensure even browning.
- Remove biscuits when they are a uniform medium brown. Place in basket lined with absorbent toweling and keep warm. Fry all of the biscuit cutouts in the same manner. Serve warm with butter and apple butter.

I'm happy to share a favorite recipe. AIDS is a very serious problem, and it will take all of us working together to come to grips with it.

My favorite recipe is a dessert recipe. (What can I do? I have a sweet tooth.)

– GUENIA LEMOS –

Strawberry Fool

INGREDIENTS

1 pint strawberries
2 teaspoons balsamic vinegar
1 cup heavy cream
⅓ to ½ cup confectioner's sugar

DIRECTIONS

- In a food processor, purée 1 cup of strawberries with the vinegar. Chop the remaining strawberries into approximately ¼-inch pieces. Combine with fruit purée.
- In a chilled medium glass or stainless bowl, whip the cream to a soft peak. Sift the confectioner's sugar into the cream and whip to a firm peak. Serve over strawberries.

Serves 4.

– GORDON THOMSON –

Favorite Recipe

DIRECTIONS

- Halve a cantaloupe.
- Remove the pulp with a melon baller.
- Smooth out the shell with a large spoon.
- Mix the melon pieces (the little balls you scooped out) with halved strawberries, seedless grapes, blueberries, or any combination of fresh fruit in bite-sized pieces with some raw sugar and a little rum if you like.
- Return the fruit mixture to the melon shells and chill for about half an hour to macerate.
- Serve cool but not cold.

Bon Apetit –
Gordon Thomson

With my warmest wishes and a big hug –
Gordon Thomson

Happy Reading!

Jackie Collins

– JACKIE COLLINS –

Orange Chocolate Cheesecake

INGREDIENTS

½ cup of cream

2 beaten eggs, room temperature

1 ½ cartons whipped cream cheese, room temperature

¾ cup sugar

2 teaspoons orange extract

½ cup finely grated orange peel

2 packs milk chocolate cookies

2 sticks butter, room temperature

1 cup sour cream

1 teaspoon orange extract

¼ cup sugar

DIRECTIONS

· Mix the cookies and 1 stick of melted butter together until a paste. Bake in a large square Pyrex dish at 450°F for 5 minutes. Remove from oven and cool.

· Mix the cream cheese, sugar, orange extract, orange peel, stick of butter, and beaten eggs and cream until well blended.

· Pour over crust and bake for 20 minutes at 350°F. Remove from oven and let cool.

· Mix 1 cup of sour cream, 1 teaspoon orange extract, and ¼ cup of sugar until blended. Pour over cake. Bake for another 5 minutes and serve cool.

– TIPPER GORE –

Tennessee Treats

INGREDIENTS

2 cups dark brown sugar (firmly packed)
2 whole eggs and 2 egg whites
2 tablespoons honey
1 teaspoon baking powder dissolved in ¼ cup
    boiling water
2 cups flour
½ teaspoon cinnamon
⅛ teaspoon allspice
⅛ teaspoon ground cloves
½ teaspoon salt
½ cup raisins
½ cup chopped dates
½ cup walnut pieces

DIRECTIONS

- Preheat oven to 350°F. In a large mixing bowl, mix brown sugar and eggs. Add honey and stir. Add baking powder to water and mix. Add water to mixing bowl. Combine flour and spices and stir into mixture. Add remaining ingredients and stir.
- Pour into greased 8 x 12-inch baking pan. Bake 350°F for 30 to 40 minutes. To determine when treats are ready, insert toothpick. A nearly dry toothpick indicates they are done. Cut into squares while warm.

I'm pleased to share the Gore family recipe for Tennessee Treats. This is one of my favorites, and I hope you will enjoy it too. Bon appétit!

Achy Breaky Cake

DIRECTIONS

- 1 yellow cake mix. Bake in 9 x 13-inch pan. When cooled, poke numerous holes in cake with straw.
- 1 can Borden condensed milk
- 1 small squeeze bottle of Smuckers or Hershey's caramel sauce. (Usually found by ice cream section in grocery store.)
- Combine milk and sauce until smooth and pour over cooled cake.
- 1 16-ounce container Cool Whip
- 2 large Butterfinger bars (crushed)
- Ice cake with Cool Whip. Sprinkle crushed Butterfingers over top. Keep refrigerated.

– MARK MILLER –

Chocolate Turbo Cake

INGREDIENTS

1 box chocolate devil's-food cake mix
1 large box instant chocolate pudding mix
1 cup oil
½ cup warm water
1 cup sour cream
4 eggs (Lisa uses only 3 eggs)
1 bag semi-sweet chocolate morsels (Nestle mini-morsels)

DIRECTIONS

- Mix all ingredients together and then fold in the mini-morsels.
- Bake in a well-greased bundt pan at 350°F for 1 hour.

It is great just out of the pan or you can top the cake by sprinkling powdered sugar on it or drizzling it with a chocolate icing.

This is Mark Miller's favorite chocolate cake recipe, provided by Mark's wife, Lisa.

Lisa said Mark loves it when he comes off the road and she has a chocolate turbo cake sitting on the counter. Enjoy! Mark and Lisa

– ANNE MURRAY –

Mom's Cherry Cake

INGREDIENTS

1 ½ cups butter

2 cups granulated sugar

4 eggs

1 teaspoon each vanilla, almond, and lemon extracts

4 cups all-purpose flour

2 teaspoons baking powder

1 teaspoon salt

1 cup milk

1 ½ cups each halved red and green candied cherries

DIRECTIONS

- With electric mixer, cream butter with sugar thoroughly. Add eggs, one at a time, beating well after each. Beat in extracts.
- Combine 3 ½ cups of flour with baking powder and salt; mix thoroughly. Add flour mixture to creamed mixture alternately with milk.
- Toss cherries with remaining ½ cup flour; fold into batter. Pour into well-greased and floured 10-inch bundt pan. Bake in a 325°F oven for 1 ¾ hours or until tester inserted in center comes out clean. Let cool a few minutes in pan and then turn out onto a wire rack to cool completely.

Chef Boy R. Dees' Lemon Lemon Pie

DIRECTIONS

- Prepare Dees' Foolproof Pie Crust first and set aside.
- Pick 2 fresh medium-sized lemons from your tree.
- Cut off the nubs at each end. Cut lemons in half. Remove the white pulp vein from the middle of each half. Grate the lemons (peel and all!). Remove seeds.
- Add 2 cups of sugar and 1 full teaspoon of pure vanilla extract.
- Cover and put in refrigerator for 7 hours or overnight.
- Beat 4 eggs and add to lemon mixture. Pour into Dees' Foolproof Pie Crust. Add top crust. Mmm!
- Bake at 350°F for about 40 minutes or until gently browned.

Dees' Foolproof Pie Crust:

4 cups all-purpose flour
1 cup shortening
¾ cup butter
1 tablespoon sugar
1 teaspoon salt
1 egg
1 tablespoon white vinegar
½ cup cold water
1 teaspoon almond extract

- Sift together flour, sugar, and salt. Cut in shortening and butter.
- Mix together egg, water, vinegar, and almond extract and combine with other ingredients. Form into a ball and chill for at least 15 minutes. Makes enough for 2 double-crust pies.

Lemon Ice Box Pie

INGREDIENTS

Juice from 2 lemons
2 egg yolks
1 can condensed milk
1 cup Cool Whip
9-inch graham cracker pie shell

DIRECTIONS

- Beat egg yolks. Slowly beat in the can of condensed milk. Add your lemon juice ever so slowly. (The lemon juice "cooks" the eggs.) Mix in ½ cup Cool Whip.
- Pour mixture into pie crust. Spread the remaining Cool Whip on top. Garnish with lemon wedges. Refrigerate for 2 hours.
- Now eat!

A cool treat from the deep South.

Gar-an-teed to please!

– JESSICA MCCLINTOCK –

Walnut Squares

INGREDIENTS

1 large egg, beaten
1 cup packed brown sugar
1 cup chopped walnuts
5 rounded tablespoons flour, sifted
1 teaspoon vanilla

DIRECTIONS

- Preheat oven to 350°F.
- Grease an 8 x 8-inch square pan.
- Combine all the ingredients and pour into the prepared pan. Bake for 20 to 25 minutes. Cool and cut in the pan while still somewhat warm. Remove from the pan when completely cool.
- Lightly dust with powdered sugar (optional).

A Jessica McClintock favorite!

Mouth-Watering Bread Pudding Not for Dieters!

Enjoy! Bill Cosby

INGREDIENTS

6 to 7 slices stale bread
1 egg, beaten
½ cup honey
1 pint half-and-half
½ pint heavy cream
1 stick butter
Dash ground nutmeg
2 teaspoons vanilla extract
Fresh grapes
Pans needed:
Pyrex dish with cover
Pan large enough to hold Pyrex dish with water in it

PREPARATIONS

- Preheat oven to 450°F.
- In a saucepan, place half-and-half, butter, heavy cream, and honey.
- Slowly heat 'til warm.
- Stir in nutmeg, vanilla extract, and beaten egg.
- Butter inside of Pyrex dish.
- Tear bread into bite-sized pieces.
- Place layer of bread and then layer of grapes, ending up with layer of bread on top.
- Pour mixture over bread/grapes (should wet all of the bread; if not, add a little milk).
- Cover dish; place in the pan of water.
- Put into 450°F oven for 10 minutes.
- Lower heat to 350°F and cook for 35 to 40 minutes.

Great hot or cold.

– CHEF RAYMOND BLANC –

Oeufs a la Neige (Floating Islands)

PLANNING AHEAD

Both the crème anglaise and the snow eggs may be made half a day in advance.

INGREDIENTS

750 ml milk
1 vanilla pod, split lengthways
6 free-range egg whites
180 grams castor sugar
8 free-range egg yolks

METHOD

- Bring the milk to a boil with the vanilla pod. Keep warm over the lowest possible heat.
- In an electric mixer on medium speed, beat the egg whites to soft peaks and then add 175 grams of the sugar little by little. When all in, increase the speed and beat until firm.
- Scoop out 8 large spoonfuls of meringue and poach 4 at a time for 2 minutes on each side in the milk at just below simmering point, turning them very gently with a slotted spoon. Remove them and allow to drain on a tray lined with absorbent paper.
- Whisk the egg yolks together with the remaining sugar in a bowl and pour in the poaching milk. Whisk together well and then return to a clean saucepan over a medium heat. Stir continuously until the mixture coats the back of a spoon. Strain immediately into a clean bowl and leave to cool and "set." Add the poached meringues to the bowl and then refrigerate for at least 4 hours.

Serve at the table for everyone to help themselves.

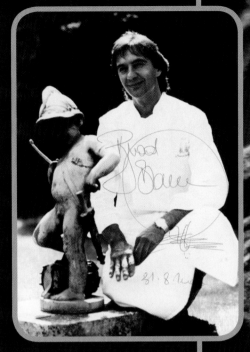

Children in France have always been an integral part of the gathering around the table, and the Floating Island, that delightful concoction, was certainly one way to keep us well-behaved and waiting for the delicious dessert.

Actually, Floating Islands is so famous that it belongs as much to the family repertoire as to cuisine you will find in any French home and in many swank restaurants.

Choc-Tini

INGREDIENTS

3 ounces melted Valhrona chocolate
6 ounces Grey Goose L'Orange vodka

DIRECTIONS

· First put Grey Goose vodka in shaker, shake 10 seconds, add chocolate, shake 10 seconds, and serve in a martini glass, leaving ½ inch to rim. Put a slice of orange on the rim.

Flute owner Herve Rousseau (left) and Francois Fourrier, manager (right).

This is a chocolate martini made with melted Valhrona chocolate prepared in the kitchen by executive chef Tom Kukoly (the chocolate is melted Bain Marie).

– CHEF DANIEL ORR –

Forest Berries in Verjus with Honey and Mint

INGREDIENTS

1 cup verjus (grape juice from sour grapes available in gourmet shops)
3 tablespoons wildflower honey
1 pinch salt
½ teaspoon sweet spices
10 mint leaves, cut chiffonade
4 cups mixed wild berries, chilled

DIRECTIONS

- Warm verjus lightly and add honey, salt, and spices.
- Mix well and adjust flavor with a little lemon or honey if needed.
- Pour syrup while warm over berries and toss with mint.
- To serve, fruit may be chilled or served straight away with a crème fraiche or vanilla ice cream. Use mint sprigs to garnish.

Serves 4 to 6.

Sherry

– CHEF SHERRY YARD –

Blueberry Financier Brown Butter Almond Cake

EQUIPMENT
Small mixing bowl
Beaters/paddle attachment
Small pot

INGREDIENTS
8 ounces (2 sticks) butter
1 fresh bay leaf
8 egg whites
8 ounces (2 cups) confectioner's sugar
4 ounces (¾ cup) all-purpose flour
4 ounces (1 cup) almond flour/meal
3 ounces (½ cup) blueberries

DIRECTIONS
- In a small pot over a medium flame, cook the butter to nutty in color. Remove from heat.
- Tear fresh bay leaf to release perfume and add the bay leaf to the hot butter.
- Allow to infuse for 5 minutes and then carefully remove from butter.
- Cool butter to room temperature or 70°F.
- Sift the all-purpose flour, confectioner's sugar, and the almond meal into a 5-quart Kitchen Aid mixer.
- Fit the mixer with the paddle attachment.
- Add the egg whites and whip on medium speed for 2 minutes. Scrape down the sides and continue to whip for 2 more minutes.
- With the mixer running, stream in the cooled butter, scraping down as you go.
- At this point you can add 1 teaspoon of cinnamon or any desired spice.
- Once butter is completely blended, whip on high speed for 2 minutes.
- Place in smell-free container and refrigerate overnight.
- The following day, whip the amount desired to "lighten up" the base and spoon into prepared pan; fill two thirds of the way. Dot with blueberries or desired fruit.
- Bake in a 350°F oven. For 4-inch individuals, bake 12 to 15 minutes; for 9-inch rounds, bake 25 to 30 minutes.

This base can be made 2 weeks in advance!

– CHEF GORDON HAMERSLEY –

Souffléed Lemon Custard©

INGREDIENTS

½ cup unsalted butter, softened
1 ½ cups sugar
6 large eggs, separated
¼ teaspoon grated lemon zest
1 cup fresh lemon juice
⅔ cups all-purpose flour, sifted
2 cups milk
1 cup heavy cream
½ teaspoon salt
Fresh mint leaves or berries for garnish

DIRECTIONS

· Preheat the oven to 350°F.
· In a large bowl, with an electric mixer on medium speed, cream the butter and sugar until fluffy.
· Add the egg yolks 1 at a time. Add the lemon juice, flour, and zest, stirring until just barely combined. Stir in the milk and cream until smooth.
· In a separate bowl, beat the egg whites until they hold soft to medium peaks, adding the salt halfway through. Fold into the custard mixture.
· Pour the custard mixture into a 10-inch round cake pan and set into a larger pan filled with 1 inch of water. Bake for about 50 minutes or until the custard is just set. Let cool to room temperature and serve garnished with mint leaves or berries.

Havana Bananas with Rhum, Chilies, and Chocolate Sauce©

INGREDIENTS

4 ripe bananas
2 ½ tablespoons butter
1 tablespoon dark brown sugar
2 tablespoons prepared chili jelly (recipe below)
3 tablespoons Meyers dark rum
4 scoops vanilla ice cream
Chocolate Sauce (recipe below)

- Peel the bananas and cut them into quarter-inch-thick slices. Heat a skillet to moderately hot. Place the bananas in the skillet with the butter and brown sugar. When the butter is melted, add the chili jelly. Toss the bananas around to coat them. Now add the rum to the pan and carefully deglaze.
- Place a scoop of ice cream onto the center of 4 shallow bowls. Arrange the bananas around the ice cream. Drizzle with warm chocolate sauce. Serve.

For the Chili Jelly:

2 ancho chilies, stems and seeds discarded
2 chipotle chilies, stems and seeds discarded
6 tablespoons red currant jelly
6 tablespoons honey
2 tablespoons Spanish sherry wine vinegar

- Toast the chili skins in a dry skillet until you can smell their earthy heat.
- Put them in saucepan with 1 quart of water and simmer on medium heat until the water is almost completely evaporated. Add the currant jelly, honey, and vinegar. Bring to a boil. Now remove from the heat and process in a food processor thoroughly. Remove to a clean bowl and cool.

For the Chocolate Sauce:

4 ounces best quality bittersweet chocolate
1 ½ tablespoons water
2 tablespoons butter

- Cut up the chocolate into small pieces and melt in a bowl with the water over simmering water. Take off the heat and whisk in the butter. Keep warm.

Serves 4.

170

German Apple Pancake with Crème Fraiche

Pancake Batter:

5 large eggs
1 tablespoon pure vanilla extract
¾ cup granulated sugar
½ cup all-purpose flour
1 ½ teaspoons baking powder

Apples:

2 tablespoons unsalted butter
3 Golden Delicious apples, peeled if desired, cored, and cut into ½-inch wedges
1 ½ teaspoons ground cinnamon
1 ½ tablespoons granulated sugar
1 tablespoon confectioner's sugar
¼ cup crème fraiche
1 cup strawberries, for garnish

- In a blender or food processor, combine the eggs, vanilla, and sugar and blend for about 15 seconds or until combined. Add the flour and baking powder and mix for 60 seconds more or until very smooth.

- Preheat the broiler to medium-high heat. Heat a 12-inch nonstick skillet over medium heat and add the butter. Add the apples and sauté for 4 to 5 minutes or until softened. Add the cinnamon and sugar, sprinkling them evenly over the apples, and stir for 2 minutes or until the apples are glazed and slightly translucent at the edges.

- Distribute the apples evenly in the skillet and pour the batter over them. (You may also make 4 individual pancakes, using a smaller pan. Just use one quarter of the apples and one quarter of the batter for each.) Cook until the bottom seems quite firm, about 8 minutes. Transfer the pan to the broiler and, while watching carefully, cook until the pancake is firm throughout and golden on top. Cut each pancake into 4 wedges and transfer them, apple side up, to serving plates. Sprinkle with the confectioner's sugar, place a dollop of the crème fraiche on top, and garnish with the strawberries.

Serves 4.

We've had these apple pancakes at Rockenwagner since we opened, and I think they are fantastic, especially for lunch. One of the things my mom cooked well was apple pancakes. She used to slice the apples into disks so that they had a little hole in the center where the core was. Then she just dipped them in the batter and pan-fried them. That's a little different than the way I like to do it now (mine is more like an upside-down apple pancake), but I have wonderful memories of her apple pancakes.

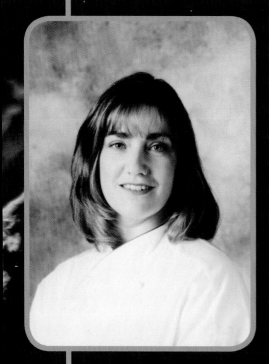

Chocolate from South America first made its way to Europe in the form of cocoa, and there was a tremendous fad when the drink was introduced to France in the seventeenth century. The Marquise de Sevigne, the most famously witty letter-writer of her era, wrote to her daughter in 1671: "If you are not feeling well, if you have not slept, chocolate will revive you. But you have no chocolate pot! I think of that again and again! How will you manage?"

Cocoa, bittersweet chocolate, and white chocolate make this pudding deep and velvety. Dutch cocoa is richer and darker than plain cocoa; it has been treated to reduce the natural acidity of the cocoa, allowing the chocolate flavor to come through more strongly without bitterness. White chocolate, of course, is not really chocolate at all but in chip form provides a wonderfully sweet counterpart to the dark chocolate.

– CHEF GALE GAND –

Triple Chocolate Custard

INGREDIENTS

1 ½ cups sugar
¾ cup cocoa powder (preferably Dutch process)
½ cup cornstarch
⅛ teaspoon (heaping) kosher salt
3 cups 2 percent milk
3 cups half-and-half
3 ounces bittersweet chocolate
2 tablespoons vanilla extract
3 ounces white chocolate, chopped with a knife or pulsed in a food processor

INSTRUCTIONS

- In a mixing bowl, whisk together the sugar, cocoa, cornstarch, and salt. In a thin stream, whisk in the milk until smooth. In a thin stream, whisk in the half-and-half and whisk until smooth.
- Pour the mixture through a fine sieve or chinois into a saucepan. Over medium heat, whisking the mixture constantly, bring to a boil. Boil gently 2 minutes. Turn off the heat and stir in the bittersweet chocolate and vanilla extract.
- Fill a large bowl with ice cubes, rest the saucepan on top, and add cold water to cover the ice cubes. Let the mixture cool, stirring frequently, about 15 minutes.
- Fold in the white chocolate and pour the mixture into 1-cup ramekins, cups, or mugs.
- Refrigerate until well chilled. (The recipe can be made through this step up to 2 days in advance.) Serve cold.
Note: Dark chocolate and wine do not harmonize; drink espresso coffee with this intense dessert.

Serves 6 to 8.

Graham Crackers

Nancy Silverton

INGREDIENTS

2 ½ cups plus 2 tablespoons unbleached pastry
   flour or unbleached all-purpose flour
1 cup dark brown sugar, lightly packed
1 teaspoon baking soda
¾ teaspoon kosher salt
7 tablespoons (3 ½ ounces) unsalted butter,
   cut into 1-inch cubes and frozen
⅓ cup mild-flavored honey, such as clover
5 tablespoons whole milk
2 tablespoons pure vanilla extract

For the Topping:
3 tablespoons granulated sugar
1 teaspoon ground cinnamon

DIRECTIONS

· In the bowl of a food processor fitted with the
steel blade or in the bowl of an electric mixer
fitted with the paddle attachment, combine the
flour, brown sugar, baking soda, and salt. Pulse
or mix on low to incorporate. Add the butter and
pulse on and off or mix on low until the mixture
is the consistency of a coarse meal.

· In a small bowl, whisk together the honey, milk,
and vanilla extract. Add to the flour mixture and
pulse on and off a few times or mix on low until
the dough barely comes together. It will be very
soft and sticky.

· Turn the dough out onto a lightly floured work
surface and pat the dough into a rectangle about
1 inch thick. Wrap in plastic and chill until firm,
about 2 hours or overnight.

To Prepare the Topping:

- In a small bowl, combine the sugar and cinnamon and set aside.
- Divide the dough in half and return half to the refrigerator. Sift an even layer of flour onto the work surface and roll the dough into a long rectangle about an eighth inch thick. The dough will be sticky, so flour as necessary. Trim the edges of the rectangle to 4 inches wide. Working with the shorter side of the rectangle parallel to the work surface, cut the strip every 4 ½ inches to make 4 crackers. Gather the scraps together and set aside. Place the crackers on 1 or 2 parchment-lined baking sheets and sprinkle with the topping. Chill until firm, about 30 to 45 minutes. Repeat with the second batch of dough.
- Adjust the oven rack to the upper and lower positions and preheat the oven to 350°F.
- Gather the scraps together into a ball, chill until firm, and reroll. Dust the surface with more flour and roll out the dough to get about 2 or 3 more crackers.
- Mark a vertical line down the middle of each cracker, being careful not to cut through the dough. Using a toothpick or a skewer, prick the dough to form two dotted rows about half inch from each side of the middle dividing line.
- Bake for 25 minutes, until browned and slightly firm to the touch, rotating the baking sheets halfway through to ensure even baking.

Yields 10 large crackers.

Fleur de Lys Chocolate Truffles

INGREDIENTS

- 14 ounces cream
- 1 tablespoon honey
- 16 ounces bittersweet chocolate, cut into small bits (¼ inch)
- 3.5 ounces unsalted butter, room temperature
- 2 tablespoons dark rum
- 5 tablespoons unsweetened cacao

Special Equipment:

- 1 tiny ice cream scoop or large melon baller (bowl of scoop about 1 inch diameter)
- 1 cookie sheet lined with parchment paper or aluminum foil
- 1 1 ½-quart heavy-bottomed saucepan plus lid
- 36 fluted paper candy cups (optional)

PREPARATION

- Put the cream and honey in a saucepan and bring to a boil. Remove from the heat and add the chopped chocolate. Cover up and let the mixture stand for 5 minutes. Then add the butter and stir with a whisk until smooth. Transfer the mixture to a small bowl and mix in the rum. Allow to cool for 30 minutes and then refrigerate for 1 ½ hours.
- Using the ice cream scoop, scoop out 1-inch balls and display them on the cookie sheet. Refrigerate for 15 minutes.
- Put the cacao in a shallow dish. Roll the chocolate balls, one-by-one, until completely covered with the cacao. Be not concerned if the chocolate truffles look slightly irregular; they will only look more authentic. Arrange them in fluted paper candy cups.

Note: There are different options to coating to enrobe the truffles: finely chopped pistachios, hazelnuts, almonds, or macadamia nuts; shredded coconut; or melted bittersweet chocolate.

Different flavors can be added: vanilla beans (split and boiled in the cream) or one or two cinnamon sticks to infuse the cream. Substitute the rum with Grand Marnier, cognac, or Eau de Vie.

Yields about 3 dozen

The dining experience at Fleur de Lys would not be complete without these little delicacies at the end of the meal. They are one of our trademarks and perennially popular, so I'm sure the reaction will be just as favorable when you serve them. Always serve the truffles at room temperature so they melt instantly in the mouth: the texture will be smooth, and the fragrance of the chocolate, rum, and honey will be much more intense. These truffles may be refrigerated for up to a week before serving. Simply store them in an airtight container. If the cocoa coating becomes absorbed during this time, just roll the truffles in some fresh cocoa powder before serving.

Enjoy!

Chocolate Chip New York Cheesecake with Chocolate Crust

INGREDIENTS

Crust:
  1 ½ cups Oreo cookie crumbs
  ½ cup melted butter

Filling:
  5 packages (8 ounces) cream cheese
  1 ¾ cups sugar
  3 tablespoons flour
  ¼ teaspoon salt
  1 teaspoon vanilla
  5 eggs (room temperature)
  2 egg yolks
  ¼ cup heavy cream
  1 cup mini chocolate chips
  Ganache Topping:
  (approximate measurements)
  1 cup chocolate chips
  ¼ cup whipping cream
  Extra mini chips to sprinkle on ganache

DIRECTIONS

Crust:
  • Combine cookie crumbs with melted butter. Press into bottom of 9-inch spring form pan. Set aside. Preheat oven to 500°F.

Filling:
  • Beat cream cheese in electric mixer until fluffy. Combine next 3 ingredients, add to cheese, and beat 1 egg at a time into mixture. After mixing add whipping cream, vanilla, and chocolate chips. Pour on top of crust in springform pan.

Bake at 500°F for 5 minutes and then turn oven to 200°F (do not open door) and bake for 1 hour. Turn off oven and leave in closed oven for 1 ½ hours or until completely cooled. Chill in refrigerator a few hours.

Ganache Topping:
- In double boiler (or over low heat) melt chocolate chips and whipping cream until medium consistency.
- Take cheesecake out of springform pan and top with warm ganache, letting ganache drip down sides all the way around. Sprinkle warm ganache with mini chocolate chips. Refrigerate again.

THIS 'N' THAT

All the best for
Dudley Moore

– DUDLEY MOORE –

squashed fly – delicious.

Good luck to all of you.
in celebrity cookbook land –
and in your efforts to get
more AIDS research moving.

Dudley Moore

180

– GEORGE BURNS –

GEORGE BURNS

TO WHOM IT MAY CONCERN:

I am lucky enough to have a very good cook who works for me. And I would not want to say anything that would upset this lovely lady. So....everything Arlette cooks is my favorite recipe.

Now that I've covered myself, I will say that if the soup is served stove hot, and I mean hot, and there is a bottle of ketchup on the table, you have a very happy George Burns.

Good luck with your book.

Sincerely,

George Burns

George Burns

P.S.   Arlette really is the greatest. I'm getting hungry just reading this letter.

Paula Poundstone's Recipe for an Airport Breakfast

INGREDIENTS

Hot dog
Diet soda

DIRECTIONS

Although for environmental reasons as well as occasional unwelcomed pangs of conscience I generally try to avoid meat, at breakfast time in an airport I do truly enjoy an airport hot dog and medium diet soda. Mr. Blanchard, my junior high history teacher, read us an article that claimed that 14 percent of hot dogs are rodent hairs and insect parts, and so I comfort myself with the thought that they may even be meat-free. As an added benefit, on the many days that I have a carry-on bag on each shoulder, getting the food, paying for it, restoring the change to my pocket, applying the condiments to the dog, and lumbering with the works to a seat at the gate to dine can, I think, count as a weight-loss program.

I go with a medium diet soda as opposed to the large tankard available because I don't like to use the bathroom on the plane if I can avoid it. The temptation to tamper with the smoke detector is too great (and, no, I do not smoke). Besides, whether you ask for Diet Pepsi and they say they only have Diet Coke or you ask for Diet Coke and they only have Diet Pepsi, at the airport the soda is the kind dispensed with a gun from the tanks, and they've managed to make it taste uniformly equi-wretched. I only even get the diet soda there in case the hot dog happens to be hot and I burn my tongue. The diet soda is a safety measure. The plastic lids can be recycled, and I carry them home to do so.

Sometimes the hot dog is actually hot, making applying the condiments particularly important. By the way, a dog properly bunned does not require a Styrofoam plate. The first few steps from the cash register to the condiment counter with a hot dog in one hand, a medium diet soda in the other, and a 30-pound bag on each shoulder are not easy, and it may be wise to practice in the home, either substituting with plastic fruit or using real food but containing the practice to a stainproof area. Ideally, the ketchup is in a large dispenser so you can get a plastic knife right near it, slice the dog down the center, hold it beneath the spout of the dispenser, and depress the big ketchup button, applying distinctive tomato-flavored coolant right up the middle of the dog. Although I often have to use the foil pouches of condiments, they are messy and wasteful and difficult to open. Sometimes it takes so long to open those foil condiment pouches (and squeeze out precious little hot dog coolant from each) using my teeth, trying not to wear it, balancing my 40 pounds of carry-on luggage on each shoulder, that a big line of impatient condiment-seeking businessmen will form behind me to reflect on the poor quality of my entire life.

By now the luggage straps, bearing 50 pounds apiece, have usually worked their way off my shoulders to my upper arms and can only be maintained by extending my elbows out from my sides. Of course, after all this work it's important not to spill, so I try to sip at the beverage while shuffling slowly toward the gate in this posture—I've never seen myself from the back, but I suppose, when I do it right, I look like a big chicken perhaps headed for a cruise.

Once at the gate, I generally find a place to dine on the floor. I kneel slowly, as if balancing an ornate tribal headdress, in order to lower my 60-pound bags and food. Of course, in cooking, presentation is very important, so I try to place the hot dog and beverage on the floor in a decorative fashion to please the eye before pleasing the palate.

I can't help it; cooking is in my blood.

– RESTAURANT LISTINGS –

Andre's
401 S. 6th St.
Las Vegas, NV 89101
702.385.5016
www.andrelv.com
Chef and Proprietor Andre Rochat

Angeli Caffe
7274 Melrose Ave.
Los Angeles, CA 90046
323.936.9086
www.angelicaffe.com
Chef/Owner Evan Kleiman

Aquavit
13 West 54th St.
New York, NY 10019
212.307.7311
Executive Chef Marcus Samuelsson

Autumn Moon Café
3909 Grand Ave.
Oakland, CA 94610
510.595.3200
www.autumnmooncafe.citysearch.com
Chef/Owner Kerry Heffernan

Cache Cache
205 South Mill St.
Aspen, CO 81611
888.511.3835
www.cachecache.com
Chef Michael Beary

Café Annie
Galleria
1728 Post Oak Blvd
Houston, TX
713.840.1111
Chef/Owner Robert Del Grande

Café Portofino
2345 Niumala Rd.
Lihue, HI 96766
808.245.2121
Owner Giuseppe Avocadi

Campanile
624 S. La Brea Ave.
Los Angeles, CA 90036
323.938.1447
Chef/Co-Owner Nancy Silverton

Drago
2628 Wilshire Blvd.
Santa Monica, CA 90403
310.828.1585
Chef/Owner Celestino Drago

East Coast Grill
1271 Cambridge St.
Cambridge, MA 02139
617.491.6568
Chef/Owner Chris Schlesinger

Fleur de Lys
777 Sutter St.
San Francisco, CA 94109
415.673.7779
Chef/Owner Hubert Keller

Flute
40 East 20th St.
New York, NY 10003
212.529.7870
www.flutebar.com
Owner Herve Rousseau

Galileo
1110 21st St., N.W.
Washington, D.C. 20036
202.293.7191
Chef/Owner Roberto Donna

Georges Blanc
01540 Vonnas-France
04.74.50.90.90
Chef/Owner Georges Blanc

George Hirsch Living It Up!
P.O. Box 655
Kings Park, NY 11754
www.chefghirsch.com
Chef George Hirsch

Good News Café
694 Main St. South
Woodbury, CT 06798
203.266.4663
Chef/Owner Carole Peck

Guastavino's
409 East 59th St.
New York, NY 10022
212.980.2455
www.guastavinos.com
Executive Chef Daniel Orr

Hamersley's Bistro
553 Tremont St.
Boston, MA 02116
617.423.2700
www.hamersleysbistro.com
Chef/Owner Gordon Hamersley

Heartbeat
149 East 49th St.
New York, NY 10017
212.407.2900
Executive Chef Michel Nischan

Kinkead's
2000 Pennsylvania Ave. NW
Washington, D.C. 20006
202.296.7700
Executive Chef/Owner Robert Kinkead

La Cachette
10506 Santa Monica Blvd.
Los Angeles, CA 90025
310.470.4992
Chef/Owner Jean Francois Meteigner

Le Grand Vefour
17, Rue de Beaujolais
75001 Paris
01. 42. 96. 56. 27
Chef Guy Martin

Le Manoir
Church Road
Great Milton
Oxford OX44 7PD
United Kingdom
01.844.27.88.81
www.manoir.com
Chef Raymond Blanc

Les Pres d'Eugenie
40320 Eugenie
Les Bains, France
05.58.05.06.07
Chef Michel Guerard

Maui Tacos
834 Front St., Suite 102
Lahaina, Maui, HI 96761
808.667.9390
www.mauitacos.com
Chef /Owner Mark Ellman

Morrison-Clark Historic Inn & Restaurant
Massachusetts Ave. & 11 St., N.W.
Washington, D.C. 20001
202.898.1200
Executive Chef Bob Beaudry

Napa Style
801 Main St.
St. Helena, CA 94574
1.866.776.NAPA
www.napastyle.com
Chef Michael Chiarello

Norman's
21 Almeria Ave.
Coral Gables, FL 33134
305.446.6767
www.normans.com
Chef/Owner Norman Van Aken

Renoir
The Mirage
3400 Las Vegas Blvd. South
Las Vegas, NV 89109
702.791.7111
www.mirage.com
Executive Chef Alessandro Stratta

Rockenwagner
2435 Main St.
Santa Monica, CA 90405
310.399.6504
Chef/Owner Hans Rockenwagner

Sign of the Sorrel Horse
4424 Old Easton Rd.
Doylestown, Bucks County, PA 18901
215.230.9999
Chef Monique Gaumont Lanvin

Spago Beverly Hills
176 North Canon Dr.
Beverly Hills, CA 90210
Chef Sherry Yard

The Blue Room
One Kendall Square
Cambridge, MA 02139
617.494.9034
theblueroom.net
Chef Jorge Lopes

The Body Gourmet, Inc.
P.O. Box 60
Venice, CA 90294
310.661.7761
www.thebodygourmet.com
Chef Jim Shiebler

The Frog and the Redneck
1423 E. Cary St.
Richmond, VA 23219
804.648.FROG
www.frogandredneck.com
Chef/Owner Jimmy Sneed

The Lark Creek Inn
234 Magnolia Ave.
Larkspur, CA 94939
415.924.7766
Chef Bradley M. Ogden

The Ritz-Carlton San Francisco
600 Stockton at California St.
San Francisco, CA 94108-2305
415.296.7465
Executive Chef Jean-Pierre Dubray

Tru
676 N. Saint Clair St.
Chicago, IL 60611
312.202.0001
Chef Gale Gand

Union Square Café
21 East 16th St.
New York, NY 10003
212.243.4020
Executive Chef Michael Romano

- INDEX -

– PHOTO CREDITS –

David Baldacci by Michael Priest

Bob Beaudry by Jim Johnson

Stephen Bishop by Lynne Goldsmith

Lane Brody by Tony Baker

Bill Clinton by The White House

Roger Clinton by Jeff Katz

Bill Cosby by Tony Esparza

Julie Dees by Harry Langdon

Rick Dees by Harry Langdon

Mark Ellman by Anthony Novak – Clifford ©
all rights reserved

Beverly Garland by Harry Langdon

Bee Gees by Anton Corbijn

Tipper Gore by The White House

Robert Del Grande by Debbie Porter

Gordon Hamersley by Betsy Cullen

George Hirsch by Hirsch Productions

Lady Bird Johnson by Frank Wolfe

Casey Kasem by Richard Armas

B.B. King by Kevin Westenberg

Bob Kinkead by Carl Cox

Diana Krall by Jane Shirek

Louise Mandrell by Rose Mason

Tim McGraw by Russ Harrington

Michel Nischan by Courtney Grant Winston

Nancy O'Dell by Associated Publications

Carole Peck by Sally Gordon – Bruce

Debbie Reynolds by Harry Langdon

Leann Rimes by Mark Liddell

Kenny Rogers by Peter Nash

Pat Sajak by Lesly Brown Sajak

Marcus Samuelson by Paul Brissman

Chris Schlesinger by Marci Joy © 1998

Jimmy Sneed by Action Photos Co., Inc.

Alessandro Stratta by Courtney Grant Winston

Elizabeth Taylor by Gary Bernstein ©

Randy Travis by Michael Tackett

Vanna White by Lesly Brown Sajak

Sherry Yard by Harry Langdon

All other photographs not listed above were used with kind permission from the selected celebrities and chefs.

– ORDERING INFORMATION –

To order additional copies of the *Celebrity Cookbook* and *Celebrity* aprons please contact the Web site at www.BonAppetitwithCelebrities.com or write to the following address. Please enclose a self-addressed stamped envelope.

Thank you.

Celebrity Cookbook
PO Box 1424
Newport Beach, CA
92659

Printed in Italy

- NOTES -

– ABOUT THE AUTHOR –

Photography by Jennifer Moss / Makeup by Tania Russell

Lisa Ann makes her debut as an author with the *Celebrity Cookbook*. She is proud to say that she has a special interest in helping people afflicted with HIV and AIDS and, as such, will be giving a percentage of the funds generated by the sales of this book to the National AIDS Fund, which is one of America's largest philanthropic organizations dedicated to eliminating HIV/AIDS as a major health and social problem through education, advocacy, and research.

Lisa, a Southern California native, began working in the entertainment field at the age of sixteen as a personal assistant to a favorite actress. This led to working with many other celebrities and working in the public relations field for the industry. In her fourteen years in this business, she has met some wonderful people.

When not writing, her favorite place to be is in the kitchen preparing great food and sharing it with friends and family. She also enjoys traveling and the theatre.

She resides in Newport Beach, California.